THE
FAMILY
BANK

Published by Mindstir Media, LLC
45 Lafayette Rd | Suite 181| North Hampton, NH 03862 | USA
1.800.767.0531 | www.mindstirmedia.com

Printed in the United States of America

ISBN-13: 979-8-9850104-1-1 (paperback)

FAMILY BANK

Life and Times of Americco L Lagomarsino

J L FOSTER

MINDSTIR MEDIA

FIRST NATIONAL BANK
SERVING THE PENINSULA

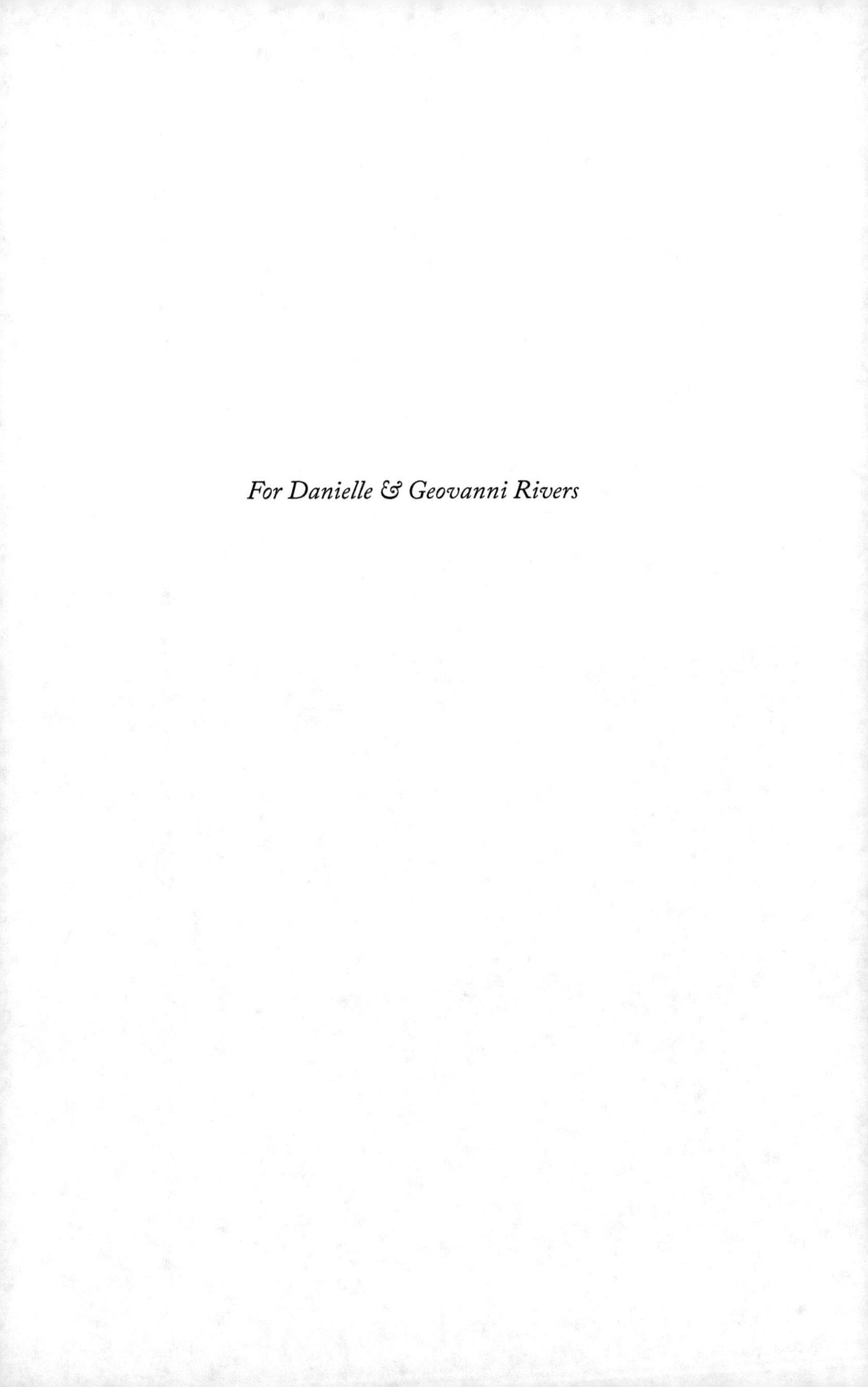

For Danielle & Geovanni Rivers

TABLE OF CONTENTS

TRUST FUND BABY

INTRODUCTION

In an age where it seems like everyone we know in business and politics is corrupt and dishonest, it's nice to know that there are still good, honest business people like my grandfather.

His name was Americco Louis Lagomarsino, but everyone knew him as "Ricco." Born on a Monday in January 1903, under the bright light of a full moon, in a one-bedroom caretaker's cottage on cemetery grounds in Colma, California. He started his life dirt poor and had no contacts or chance of success, with only a limited education. Not even he could have ever imagined of great success his achievements in life would bring to his family.

He was a self-made man with only pure willpower and determination to guide him to success. As his granddaughter, it's my honor to share his story with the public, feeling that I was put on this earth to tell a generation about my grandfather's journey from rags to riches. His story is very personal to me, not only because he is my grandfather, but I want future generations to know this great man and his legacy. It's only proper to give Americco credit for his work. For Americco's legacy would be one to last over one hundred years and beyond. Here is his story.

THE LAGOMARSINO FAMILY

Colma, California, is where my grandfather's story begins. Or maybe it starts with my great-grandparents, Louis Aratta and Teresa Lagomarsino, in Genoa, Italy, in the 1890s, a time when there was no work and people were starving in the streets.

During that time Italy was experiencing some social and political changes; and so a lot of families moved to different countries.

When Louis Aratta was in his early twenties, he married Teresa Lagomarsino. It was common in the 1890s to marry young. After they were married, my great-grandparents, along with other relatives, decided to try their luck and join the waves of immigrants traveling by boat to America.

At the time, advertisements for ship tickets promised luxury accommodations and hours of carefree pleasure, but many travelers ended up on whaling ships. My great-grandparents decided to come anyway, aboard one of the more than five hundred ships that set out to California during that time. Having secured jobs in Colma as a groundskeeper and housekeeper for the family who owned the Olivetti Cemetery, my great-grandparents thought sailing to America was an excellent opportunity. They were very fortunate to have jobs waiting for them, promised by their family members already living in Colma California . It would be a new beginning for the couple to move so far from home in Italy.

My mother would tell me how her grandparents had to travel around "the horn," though at the time, I had no idea what "around the horn" meant. Since then, I've learned that traveling by ship from Italy to San Francisco required going all the way around Cape Horn in South America, which could take up to six months. The ship ticket cost one hundred to three hundred dollars. It was an exhausting trip with rough storms, seasickness, and a lack of fresh water, fruit, and vegetables. Passengers had to eat preserved meat, fish, dried beans, potatoes, and rice. To flavor the bad-tasting water, they added molasses, vinegar, and spices to make a drink called switchel. After a few weeks on the ship, all the passengers had left was molding food.

When Teresa and Louis arrived in San Francisco in the early 1890s, they were two of the over three hundred thousand Italians who would come to America during that time. Rather than live in San Francisco's "Little Italy," they settled in Lawndale, also known as Colma, located between Daly City and South San Francisco. It was in Colma that my great-grandparents came to work for the owners of the Olivetti Cemetery, which were established in 1896. Louis worked as a groundskeeper, and Teresa worked as a house-keeper. The city of Colma and the work at the cemeteries would play a significant role in the lives of the Lagomarsino family.

In the late 1850s, Colma was just a region of north San Mateo County, almost ten miles south of the San Francisco line. Colma encompassed all the land from the summit of San Bruno Mountain to the Pacific Ocean. Back then, Colma was a farming community with flower greenhouses and fields.

Colma is believed to be an Ohlone word, meaning "many springs." But that's not what the town became known for or why my great-grandparents ended up there. In 1849, the California Gold Rush brought hundreds of thousands to San Francisco, and with them, they also brought disease leading to a high death rate. The overwhelming rate of death forced the city of San Francisco to look outside the city limits for land to bury their dead.

That high death rate made Colma unique in California; there is no other town like it in the world. Colma is sometimes called the City of Souls or City of the Dead because it was created for the sole purpose of protecting the rights of the departed. People would laugh and say " I'm dying to be in Colma?", because 90% of the people there are dead!"

Though it was not incorporated until 1924, it was established in 1887 as part of San Francisco's cemetery system to solve an enduring problem: where to bury the city's dead when the land within the city limits was too valuable for cemetery use.

The southern end of Colma was chosen because of transportation. There was easy access by horse and carriage from Mission Street, streetcars ran between San Francisco and Colma, and trains ran alongside the cemeteries. Most of those trains had stopped at each cemetery.

The official slogan of this quaint and curious town proclaims, "It's great to be alive in Colma!" In no other city in the United States would such a slogan have the meaning that it does here. Colma, only 2.25 square miles, has fifteen hundred living residents but a thousand times more in its deceased population.

Interred in Colma are human and animal souls resting eternally in the sixteen cemeteries of this tiny town. One of the famous inhabitants of Colma cemeteries is newspaperman William Randolph

Hearst, locked inside an expensive unmarked tomb with a half-empty bottle of Evian. Nearby are dead clowns, Alcatraz inmates, a potato chip king, and lawman Wyatt Earp. It's hard to determine if any of the Lagomarsino brothers ever buried anyone famous, but it's possible.

Many devoted Catholics—including my great-grandparents—are also interred at Holy Cross Cemetery, as well as several notable historical figures, such as Joe DiMaggio, former professional baseball player. The thirty-seventh Mayor of San Francisco George Moscone, who was assassinated by Dan White, is interred at Holy Cross Cemetery. Also, the thirty-second Governor of California, Pat Brown, is resting in peace at Holy Cross Cemetery.

Within a few years of arriving in Colma and beginning work at the cemetery, my great-grandparents had a son named Fred Lagomarsino, born in 1895. After Fred came William Lagomarsino in 1899, and two years later, in 1901, George Lagomarsino arrived. My grandfather was born in January 1903 with the given name of Americco Louis Lagomarsino. According to the census in 1910 and 1920, my great-grandmother had five births, but only four children survived.

Interestingly, my great-grandmother gave all her sons her last name of Lagomarsino, rather than her husband's name of Aratta. After learning that they did not take their father's last name, I wondered why. My mother had said that the name Lagomarsino was the name of the town that Teresa was from, and I found it was common in Italy to name children after their mother's hometown in Italy if she didn't want to give her children the father's name. Later, I learned the reason why my great-grandmother did not want her sons to carry their father's name. It was interesting to find the origins of my grandfather's family name came from his mother and not his father.

When my grandfather was three years old, a massive earthquake shook San Francisco, California, on the morning of the eighteenth of April 1906. Though the quake lasted less than a minute, it was felt all the way in Colma. The quake's immediate impact was disastrous. There were fires all around the city that burned and destroyed hundreds of city blocks and most people lost their lives.

The San Francisco 1903 earthquake increased the numbers of deceased in the Colma cemeteries significantly. The increase of work at the graves meant there was never a lack of jobs in Colma for the Lagomarsino family. Americco was very young when he saw the large number of homeless people after the earthquake. I believe it led to his vision later in life to build affordable single-family homes in Daly City.

Not long after the 1906 earthquake, my great-grandfather left the family, and Teresa became the solid foundation for her sons as they grew up in Colma. My great-grandmother learned that Louis had unfaithful to her and had been having sexual relations with prostitutes. The entertainment available catered to men in the Red Light District which was called the San Francisco Barbary Coast; and Louis was one of them. Teresa must have already had concerns about the man she had married when she named her sons, but when my great-grandmother learned he had infected her with syphilis, she wanted him to leave the family so that she could raise her sons without the awful influence of their father's destructive ways.

My great-grandfather left San Francisco and sailed to Brazil, where he died in a tragic accident, an alcoholic and a womanizer to the end of his life. My great-grandmother would say she had "washed her hands of that man" and never looked back on her marriage to my great-grandfather.

Contracting syphilis at the turn of the century was a death sentence for anyone who had the illness because there was no safe cure during this time. Syphilis was a public health hazard in the 1900s and still subject to sometimes over-the-top medical responses. The only actual treatment for syphilis was not safe and was sometimes almost as damaging as the disease itself. It was mercury, eaten, inhaled, and rubbed into the skin. By the 1800s, people were not ignorant of what mercury could do to a person, but no other treatment seemed to work as well. Patients were exposed over and over until their symptoms cleared up, or they died from the insanity and rotting flesh syphilis caused.

Today, syphilis is minor and treatable with penicillin with a favorable success rate, but not in my great-grandmother's days. Teresa's only option was to continue being the capable, confident, and independent woman she was and raise her sons to be the best men in their community. My great-grandmother had to be healthy emotionally for my grandfather and his brothers, working long hours and making sure they could attend school even while she was sick and tired. Syphilis would physically affect my great-grandmother for the rest of her life, not to mention the social stigma attached to people having this disease. Teresa did the best she could give her circumstance with her medical condition.

My great-grandmother worked hard so that my grandfather and his brothers could attend school in Daly City. The only school in the area, Jefferson Elementary consisted of grades from first to eighth. My grandfather and his brothers were excellent students; they were happy to be attending school for as long as they could. It's amazing how brilliant, intelligent, industries and resourceful Americco and his brothers were for their time, especially without a high school or college educations.

My grandfather and his brothers were not able to participate in high school in their area. San Francisco was the only city that had secondary schools, and a few students from Colma could afford to go there. My grandfather and his brothers were not from one of those families that could send their kids to school in the city. While living in Colma, my grandfather graduated from the eighth grade at the age of twelve in 1915.

Americco would become a member of the cemetery workers' union, holding the post of secretary in 1924. He would become a leader in his union to help make working conditions better for all workers. Americco's position in the union would be the beginning of a long career of leadership in the community. My mother had told me once she thought my grandfather could have been mayor of Daly City if he wanted to enter politics. It has always perplexed me how Americco and his brothers could be visionaries so far ahead of their time even without obtaining higher educations.

At a young age, my grandfather was already responsible, accountable, and respected by almost everyone he knew in town. I remember once when I was a young girl, my grandfather was pulled over by a police officer while driving down Hillside Drive in Colma. After the police officer asked my grandfather for his driver's license and realized who he pulled over, the officer let my grandfather go without a traffic ticket. The police in his town had respect for my grandfather: he was a man you trusted to protect your money and life!

Louise Loretta Lagomarsino

FUNERAL
FOR TERESA

When my grandfather was twenty-five years old, his dear mother, Teresa Lagomarsino, left the earth. My grandfather and his brothers were left to fend for themselves entirely.

Before her death, once Teresa could no longer work because of the effects of syphilis, Americco and his brothers would take shifts caring for their mother while working their full-time jobs. Caring for their mother was never difficult for the brothers. They tried to make the end of her life as peaceful as possible, ensuring she had the two most important things to her: her church community and sons who would live a more respectable life than their father had.

My mother would tell the story of the promise all the Lagomarsino boys made to my great-grandmother that they would be better men than my great-grandfather. It was during those last days, spent saying goodbye, that they assured her they would make her proud. My great-grandmother kept reminding her boys that if they did not live a clean and honest life, they could end up like their father.

If watching their mother die was not enough to make them better men, then nothing would, she must have thought. Knowing how much grief and sorrow their father produced in their mother's life and on her health, the brothers promised her to treat their wives and children with love and respect. My grandfather and his brothers would continue to be devoted Catholics, active in their church, loyal to their families, and responsible for their business practices. Each one of them would make their mother proud by growing up as reasonable men and becoming nothing like their father.

Having been a devoted Catholic all her life, it was necessary for Teresa to interred in a Catholic cemetery. Even though my great-grandparents never worked at Holy Cross Cemetery, Teresa had made sure that her sons knew her last wishes for her funeral. So, she was interred at Holy Cross Catholic Mausoleum on 1500 Mission Road in Colma, the oldest and largest cemetery in "the city of cemeteries."

What was a farm then became Holy Cross Cemetery

It was a testament to her sons' love for her that my great-grandmother was interred at one of the nicest cemeteries in Colma. Teresa's date of death listed as the seventh of July 1928. Her birth certificate date was 1874, so she was fifty-four years old when she died. However, the headstone incorrectly reads 1854 as her date of birth. I don't know why the headstone was never changed to the correct date, but it might have been the fact the headstone was too costly to correct. It is a shame that the stonecutter's mistake on her headstone will be there for eternity, and it's noteworthy to document the error for future generations.

THE TEALDI FAMILY

The ship that Elia Tealdi sailed aboard was named *La Gascogne*. It was a French steel-hulled ship built by Forges & Chantiers de la Mediterranee in La Seyne, France, and was in service from 1887 until 1920, at which point it was broken up for scrap. This ship was probably like the one my great-grandparents also crossed the ocean aboard. It was significant in my grandparents' time to know how your family traveled to America.

Like my great-grandparents, Elia Tealdi's destination was San Francisco, California, and just like my great-grandparents, the Tealdi family ended up in Colma, too. The similarities between the families do not end there as my great-grandparents' families were all from Castiglione Chiavarese.

Elia Tealdi had to work for over four years in America before he had enough money to send for his wife and three daughters. Finally, my great-grandmother, Dolores Raggio Rossi Tealdi and her three daughters, Ellia, Eleanor, and Marie, arrived in San Francisco in November 1913. They sailed from Genoa, Italy.

After arriving in New York, my great-grandmother and her daughters were processed at Ellis Island, which was typical for the time. From New York, Dolores Tealdi and her three daughters took a train cross-country to San Francisco, California.

My grandmother was not a naturalized citizen until she married her husband and petitioned for citizenship in January 1932. I had always assumed that my grandmother was born in Colma, and I was surprised to find out differently. I suspect my grandfather ulti-mately convinced her to become a citizen and helped her complete the necessary paperwork. It was vital during this time to become United States citizens as soon as you were legally able to.

The Tealdi family lived in a small two-bedroom house on B Street in Colma. There was a still in the garage for making wine. Back in those days, there were just dirt roads in Colma and no fences between houses. In addition to cemeteries, the town of Colma also consisted of pig farms, dairies, and open fields of cabbages and primrose flowers.

The Tealdi Family Nursery was founded in 1912 before Marie arrived from Italy. The Tealdi's owned greenhouses in Colma that provided flowers to the San Francisco Flower Market and the cemeteries. The family would become part of the San Francisco Floral Society.

The Tealdi children consisted of two sons and five daughters. After arriving from Italy, my great-grandparents had four more children: Leo in 1915, Matilde in 1917, Johnny in 1918, and Yolanda in 1923, all born in Colma, California. They all grew up in the nursery business and helped grow, sell, and distribute local flowers.

Growing and picking the flowers to sell at the Flower Market in San Francisco was a great job. The Tealdi family would take all day to travel by horse and carriage with their flowers to sell in San Francisco. It also meant that as teenagers, the Tealdi children's playground was vast. They roamed from Fleishhacker pool to the Cliff House Restaurant off Ocean Beach, from the church in the North Beach to walking up and down Mission Street to shop.

As a child, Marie would chase rabbits and birds while working at the nurseries. Marie's family had little money, her only doll made of straw. My grandmother would tell me the story of how she cried when she lost her toy in a haystack, trying to make me appreciate all the toys she gave to her children and grandchildren.

Elia and Dolores had a natural mind for business and selling flowers. Elia would always tell his children, "The pencil is stronger than the shovel" and "Use your mind, not your back, to make your money." Because he was a sharp businessman, the Tealdi family lived through the Great Depression, learned how to survive, and saved for the future.

Americco & Marie Lagomarsino

Americco & Marie Lagomarsino Wedding

THE COURTSHIP AND MARRIAGE OF AMERICCO & MARIE LAGOMARSINO

Before the Great Depression, Marie Tealdi and Americco met through her older sister, Ellia Tealdi, and her husband, Louis Bacigalupi, the local friendly barber. My grandfather knew of the Tealdi family from Colma, and he was good friends with Johnny and Leo Tealdi, Marie's brothers. When he started dating Marie, she still needed a chaperone, and so they would double date with Ellia and Louis.

Americco knew he wanted to marry Marie early in the relationship, but he was six years older and had to wait until she was old enough to date. Marie and her sisters looked stylish and dressed well, wearing pin curls in their hair. Marie was my grandfather's confidante and muse in his life. He enjoyed making Marie's life comfortable, just as he wished he could have spoiled his mother. Why they fell in love is obvious: they were a nice-looking couple, both rich in Italian history, and sought to provide for their family.

While Americco and Marie were dating, he would take her to the attractions that only San Francisco could offer. Ocean Beach in San Francisco once had a boardwalk called Playland—the Fun House with a laughing mechanical fat lady, rollercoaster rides, and a carnival atmosphere with the smells of corndogs and cotton candy in the air.

Lake Tahoe and Reno were both favorite places to take a four-hour drive in Americco's Cadillac. Both enjoyed going to Lake Tahoe in the summer and the winter to see snow in the Serra Mountains. The casinos provided entertainment, gambling, and good dining. The hotels provided a swimming pool for Marie to sunbathe in her bathing suit. Both my grandparents were in good shape and loved the outdoors.

They had so much in common growing up in Colma with their traditional Italian culture. I would often hear my grandparents talking to each other. It was like they had their own language, and they did—it's called Italian. Both came from traditional Italian Catholic families and believed marriage was important.

Remembering my grandfather, I know that he was always a gentleman when it came to his wife and family. Americco always pulled out chairs for Marie. He always opened the door for her when getting in the car.

My grandparents married on the fourth of May 1930 at Saints Peter and Paul Church at Filbert Street in San Francisco's North Beach neighborhood. They chose that church because it was known as "the Italian Cathedral of the West" and served as the cultural center for San Francisco's Italian American community for generations.

Even today, Saints Peter and Paul Church has a grand outer appearance, with two towers and a slanted cathedral roof. It looks like a magnificent castle from the Renaissance era with three crosses atop the points of the roof. Inside, the church is beautiful, with the grand religious design, stained glass, and gorgeous paintings that adorn the church, in addition to marble and other decorative stones used throughout. The altar is gorgeous and weighs a huge amount. The central platform has white marble and beautiful statues. The high writing overhead of the picture of Jesus is holding the Bible. The Greek letters read "Jesus Christ conquers."

My grandmother Marie looked like an angel on her wedding day. Her headdress even looked like she was wearing a halo with curls in her hair. She had a beautiful glow about her like all excited women on their wedding day. Louis and Ellia Tealdi-Bacigalupi's young son—Louis Bacigalupi, Jr.—was the ring bearer. Ellia was Matron of Honor, and Louis was a groomsman; Eleanor was a bridesmaid, and Yolanda was the flower girl. My great-uncle William Lagomarsino was the Best Man.

The bridal party all wore hats, as was the custom. The men wore the customary black tuxedo with carnations pinned to the lapel. My grandfather's new bride's family provided the fantastic array of flowers that the bride and her bridesmaids carried. The women all looked terrific in their twenties-style flowing gowns.

Marie's father, Elia Tealdi, walked his daughter down the aisle and gave his daughter away with Dolores by his side. Many friends and family attended their wedding, and people would say, "They made a beautiful couple." They were simply happy to have found one another and were looking forward to spending a lifetime together and raising their family in Daly City.

My grandparents' wedding day was the most important day of their life. Americco married his soulmate, the love of his life. Their marriage would be the sturdy foundation that would build and support our family, enduring for their lifetimes and beyond.

My grandparents' marriage had the kind of love and respect that is hard to find and that many people can only dream of having with a partner. They were very much in love, and it was a match made in heaven. Americco was a fortunate man to be married to the most capable, smart, beautiful woman he had ever known.

My grandfather would always make sure that my grandmother was taken care of and all her needs were met. An example of how much my grandfather loved Marie was how he treated her like a princess, just like he had promised his mother he would do all those years before. He enjoyed doing things for Marie because he wanted her to have a better life than his mother.

Americco would employ a maid named Frida who would come in once a week and clean the apartment for my grandmother. He made sure Marie had an account at the local butcher's on Mission Street, where they would give all the children a hot dog when my grandmother ordered meat. He also made sure my grandmother always had a credit card for every major store in the shopping mall, at a time when a woman couldn't have a credit card unless her husband approved it. He also made sure Marie would not need to work the way his mother did, and he worked hard to be a good provider, unlike his father.

When he was away, my grandfather would write letters to Marie to let her know she was always on his mind. Even if he had only gone so far as Napa, where he would be selling insurance, he would write Marie letters telling her to take care of herself and that he was looking forward to taking her out on a date.

My grandfather's only luxury would be a new Cadillac every year for himself or my grandmother. One year he brought her a purple Cadillac, a car I will always remember. When my grandfather or grandmother bought a new car, they gave the older car to their daughters. Being good parents to their daughters meant making sure they had not only everything to survive but luxuries too.

I remember my mother saying once that my grandmother had always wanted to live in a house and not an apartment over the office. But my grandfather could not stand the thought that he would be far away from his family instead of walking down the stairs every day to go to work. Working and taking care of his family was the most critical job my grandfather could have in life.

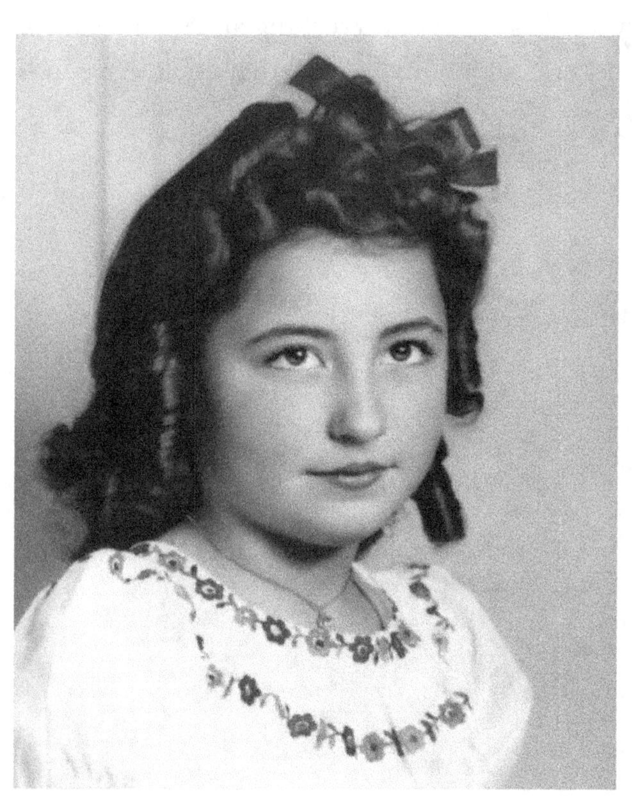

THE LAGOMARSINO DAUGHTERS

My grandparents had two daughters who were born in the 1930s. Dolores was their first daughter, and soon after, Louise Loretta, their youngest daughter, was born. Both girls were the loves of their parents' lives as they were a close family, rich in Italian traditions.

Dolores Marie was born in December 1934 at San Francisco hospital. My mother, Louise Loretta Lagomarsino, was born in May 1938 in the same San Francisco hospital via C-section. Dolores was taller and lighter-skinned than Louise Loretta, and though they both had dark hair and eyes, everyone said Dolores looked like my grandfather while Louise Loretta had all Marie's trademark looks. In fact, Louise Loretta looked so much like her mother Marie that it was sometimes hard to tell them apart.

During this time, my grandparents were living at 209 F Street in Colma. In the small house where both my mother and aunt would start their life in Colma. My mother would tell me stories about being a little girl during World War II and having air raids and being so scared at night during that time or how they would sit on the couch with their parents as they all waited for the airs raids to be over. My grandfather and his brother never served but they did serve on the draft board during the war years.

The daughters would spend most of their childhoods in their new home above my grandfather's office in Daly City, where they moved in the 1940s. The Mission Street office and apartments were my mother's home until she married. Her playground was the lot next door, which served as the family's garden. Americco built a custom playhouse in the middle of the yard for their daughters, and they had a beautiful garden with plants from all around the world.

The daughters were raised in the Catholic Church in Colma at Holy Cross on San Pedro Road. Louise Loretta had a natural ability for singing and would sing in the church choir. She would also find small jobs singing at weddings in the church, performing songs like *"Ave Maria."* My mother would tell me that she wanted to be a nun when she was a little girl. That was how much she loved being in church when she was younger.

One of my grandparents' traditions was that every Sunday, after mass, the whole family would shop at the bakery next to the church. Louise Loretta always wanted a cupcake for ten cents and would eat it all before arriving home.

During the time when both daughters were growing up, they would like to roller skate up and down the sidewalk. One day Louise Loretta was roller skating and broke her arm. She would always tell me how my grandfather scooped her up and took her to the hospital, where the doctor put a cast on her arm—another example of how well my grandfather took care of his family.

My mother would also tell me about when her father would come home from work, and my mother and her sister would run down a long hallway to the front door as soon as they heard him coming up the stairs. When my grandfather would open the door, he would swoop them up with two arms and carry them down to the living room and sit with them on his big chair and ottoman telling them about his day.

My mother also loved to talk about how much she liked to listen to her father talk about his workday around the dinner table while Marie cooked her favorite Italian recipes. Marie made the best Italian food, and she handed down her family dishes to her daughters and granddaughters. Many dishes would become family favorites for Christmas and Thanksgiving. All meals were rich in Italian heritage like homemade ravioli, lasagna, rice torta, and zucchini and spinach frittata.

My grandparents were happy that both their daughters Dolores and Louise Loretta attended Jefferson High School in Daly City. Both girls were excellent students throughout their school experience. Louise Loretta would excel in the theater and even star in the high school production of *Carmen*.

Dolores liked applying makeup, and she would wear a fake mole on her cheek, trying to look like Elizabeth Taylor. Dolores loved makeup so much she once got caught stealing lipstick from the five and dime. Americco was not proud of Dolores and her stealing when he had the means to provide her with anything she wanted.

Because my grandfather was such a good provider, my mother and aunt were happy as they grew up—for the most part. They lived right up the street from Jefferson High School during their school days, and they were active members of the Holy Cross Catholic Church, where they attended religious schooling by the Catholic Nuns. The Holy Cross Church and Cemetery and Mary's Help Catholic Hospital would become an even more significant part of my grandfather's family's life in his later years.

WM. LAGOMARSINO
& COMPANY

Even before my grandfather and his brother William decided to build their own office and apartment building, they sold insurance door-to-door at night. For over twenty years, they worked in a graveyard all day and sold life insurance at night.

The way my grandfather told it, all the brothers wanted out of the cemetery business. It was never their intention to work the rest of their lives as gravediggers. Selling insurance every night was not for the community only but was also an opportunity for the brothers to grow their business plan.

Americco and William wanted to go into business together and build an empire beyond anything anyone could imagine so they could stop relying on others to employ them and help them provide for their families. They dreamed of expanding their business, opening a one-stop shop that would meet all their customers' needs in real estate, property management, tax returns, and accounting services. The company they started is what would become William Lagomarsino & Company.

The brothers decided they would only work six days a week. On Sundays, they would go to church and take a long ride in the car to the countryside. That was how, with only determination and willpower, they managed to work hard at two jobs, which paid off because the business brought my grandfather and his brother great success and served as a stepping-stone for all their future achievements.

Selling insurance, my grandfather and his brother met many people in their community and formed a stable bond with everyone in Colma and Daly City. Their customers were barbers, cemetery workers, plumbers, carpenters, nursery workers, firefighters, welders, police officers, butchers and bakers, people from every walk of life. They were friends and associates who became lifelong customers. Americco and William became known as men of endurance in business according to the book Images of America of Daly City—the kind of men their clients would entrust a lifetime of business.

When the Great Depression ended, my grandparents lived on F Street in Colma in a small house with two daughters under five years old. They knew it was time for a more significant home and office for their family and business, and William agreed.

William and his wife, Anna, had married in the late 1930s and were having trouble finding a place to live. Finally, at age thirty-five, William and my grandfather left their cemetery jobs in Colma to focus on their own business. My grandfather used to tell how, on the day he quit, the owners of the cemetery in Colma told him, "You will never be successful in business in your life." This insult would guide his life, and later his former employer would find out they were dead wrong to doubt his abilities, and eventually, they would follow him by investing in his future business.

With their business planned, their next step was to design and contract to build their future office and home. It was the 1940s, and they chose 7100 Mission Street to be their next home for their families and business. The location was perfect on the corner of Mission Street and West Molke Street in Daly City. This location would provide the ideal frontage for a commercial business on Mission Street and would have considerable traffic for a new company.

They did not just buy the lot; they purchased the whole corner block of Mission Street and West Molke Street in Daly City to be their office and apartment. Being a man of great vision into the future, my grandfather was always thinking of ways of increasing his holdings. Acquiring blocks of property at a time was nothing new for the Lagomarsino brothers.

After blueprints, permits, and financing were approved, the construction was the next step. The design was art deco which was extremely fashionable in the 1940s era. The structure consisted of a two-story mixed-use building, with commercial space on the bottom floor and residential on the top floor. The brothers' office would be on the first floor, and the two apartments on the second floor would be where their families would live.

William and Anna would take the one-bedroom unit, and my grandparents would live in the two-bedroom apartment with a concrete and glass patio between the two apartment units. There would be a small studio apartment on the lower level over the garage to rent out for future income.

The offices would include a large wooden counter where my grandfather and William could serve their customers. The end of the counter included a waist-high swing door for easy access to the back office. With its ample office space, the bottom floor made it possible for them to house many cubicles with desks, chairs, phones, typewriters, and adding machines. Their large back office was built for conferences and meetings with clients.

My mother was about two years old when her family moved into their new building on Mission Street in Daly City. Living above my grandfather's new office building provided him with the ability to walk downstairs every morning to work. There are not many people today who can say their commute is a walk downstairs to their office unless it is in their house.

After my grandfather and his brother worked a full day at the office, I can remember my grandfather coming home from work, and my grandmother always had his dinner and a drink waiting for him. My grandparents would spend Sunday morning before church in their bedroom with the Sunday newspaper all over the bed. Maintaining their tradition of keeping Sundays as family days, I can still remember my sisters and me asking our grandparents to read us the Sunday funnies comic strips—*Blondie* and *Archie* were our favorites.

My grandparents and his brother and sister-in-law had a relationship that many people thought was like the one between the Ricardos and the Mertzes on the show *I Love Lucy*. Just like the Hollywood couples, my grandparents and his brother and his wife traveled together and lived as neighbors with nothing but glass and concrete patio between them.

Many times, as a child, I would come to visit only to find the four of them laughing as they told stories of the times they had traveled together, like when they drove to New York City. I can picture my grandparents and great-uncle and great-aunt traveling—the women sitting in the back seat talking, while my grandfather and his brother sat in the front, my grandfather driving the whole way cross-country. "He just loved being behind the wheel," my grandmother would say. "And he was such a good driver." To which my aunt would laugh and say, "No—he just liked being in the *driver's* seat, making all the decisions!"

During the trip, I'm sure my grandfather would have told the ladies in the back seat—just like he used to do with me and my sisters when he'd drive us home— to "duck down in their seats" so that he could spit out the window without getting them wet. After, the ladies talked more about the fact that the spit almost hit them in the face than they spoke of their cross-country trip from San Francisco to New York City, which would have been a once-in-a-lifetime trip for anyone during that time or even today.

That's just one small example of the relationship they shared—and it illustrates the unbreakable bond between all four of them. Not only were the brothers business partners until the end of their lives, eventually owning more than one hundred pieces of property together, but the four of them did nearly everything together.

Besides the warmth and laughter that filled the house, one of my favorite memories of my grandfather was when I was a little girl and would visit my grandfather's office. Americco was always bigger than life to me, yet he still had a smile on his face and was in a good mood when I came to see him. I never saw my grandfather get angry once, and I never saw anyone get mad at him. He was never rude or bitter at anyone or anything; there was always good karma surrounding him and our family. I felt nothing but love from my grandfather, and that is why he is my hero! He was the sweetest, warmest, sincerest, trustworthy, and the best man I have ever met in my life! No one can ever match my grandfather and the gentleness, love, respect, and gratitude he showed to our family.

His customers would always say that he was the most gracious man, and that was my experience too. When I was a little girl, our family attended an Easter Day brunch at Nick's Restaurant by the sea in Rockaway Beach. After eating our brunch, we all walked to the lower end of the parking lot, where a concrete sea wall separated the beach from the lot. As I stood by the sea wall looking over the ocean, my bow flew off my head and onto the beach. My grandfather walked all the way over the sea wall and onto the beach to return my bow to me for my hair. I will never forget the kindest he would show to his grandchildren without anyone asking him to do it.

Americco treated everyone the way he would want other people to handle him. In a time when so many professionals get away with lying and stealing from their customers and remain in business, my grandfather was different. His reputation meant everything to him, primarily when he was representing other people's interests in any market. He cultivated the image he wanted to portray, not just in how he acted but also in how he dressed. Americco always wore a three-piece suit with a coat and tie. His shoes were always shined and polished, and he wore a carnation on his coat lapel. His black hair was slicked back, and his face clean-shaven.

These are all reasons Wm. Lagomarsino & Company would thrive as a business in the 1940s and beyond. When any customer would walk into the office, they were greeted with a smile from my grandfather—the same smile he had for me.

It was a great experience watching how well he would communicate with his customers about their business needs and how he would provide the smallest touches to show he cared about their business and them. The office would give away free calendars for the customers and candy for the children. In the back office was a water cooler with hot and cold water, which we thought was so cool. My cousins were always asking for drinks from it, and Americco never minded that we wanted water or a piece of candy from the office.

When growing up, I enjoyed sitting in the big chairs behind his large wooden desk and wondering what it would be like to work with my grandfather. I would spin around in the chair, looking at the large counter at the front where the customers would do business. I loved how the large storefront picture windows said *Wm. Lagomarsino & Company* in big black and gold letters that faced Mission Street. I would think about how big everything looked behind the office counter. There were too many desks and cubicles to count when I was visiting my grandfather's office, and though I didn't know exactly how many people worked for my grandfather, I knew there were a lot of employees.

Americco was the front man of the office. With his approachable personality, it was comfortable for customers to talk business with him. At work, William was more reserved, and he liked to remain quiet in the office behind the counter or desk. Americco was the social butterfly of the family, never having a problem speaking to one person or a crowd of people. It was that quality that, of all the brothers in Americco's family, would make him the most successful in business and life.

TERESA TERRACE

Making something out of nothing was never impossible for Americco, but at the same time, my grandfather would always tell us, "It's one thing to make money; it's another thing to keep it!" One of my grandfather's first money-making projects was a subdivision in Daly City named "Teresa Terrace," in honor of his mother. She had left the property to him and his brother, hoping they would develop it. The development would be a unique project my grandfather would be proud to own and produce. Americco would tell his grandchildren how his mother saved all their extra money from working at the cemeteries to pay for the property. To think that they all lived on the cemetery grounds in a small caretaker's cottage—four sons and their mother—it's hard to imagine how challenging it must have been for Teresa to save enough money to buy that property.

Just like his mother, my grandfather never shied away from challenges. One such challenge was when he decided to obtain his contractor's licenses in the 1950s to become the general contractor of Teresa Terrace. My grandfather always said, "Having a large construction crew building new homes in the subdivision was a dream come true." Americco would tell us how proud his mother would have been knowing they had created the subdivision in her honor, how Teresa would have loved to have owned one of the homes for herself. And my grandfather was so proud that my mother would end up owning two homes in the subdivision, where I lived from birth until kindergarten.

Teresa Terrace would consist of tract homes on the first, second, and third avenues. The first two avenues consisted of fifty-three lots of single-family homes with two bedrooms, one bathroom, and full basements. The third-avenue block would include twenty-five buildable lots for single-family residential homes with three bedrooms, two bathrooms, and full basements. The single-family homes were built on lots of approximately three thousand square feet. All the houses had a backyard with fully fenced and gated yards.

In addition to supervising the subdivision itself, my grandfather managed the construction yard at one end of the development, close to Hillside Boulevard. The construction yard consisted of an old steel barn with cobblestones and dirt flooring. There was a big sign at the construction yard with a billboard advertising *Wm. Lagomarsino & Company*. The giant billboard sign towered over the barn and construction yard in big red and white letters.

Developing the subdivision and the construction company was one of the many opportunities that showed my grandfather's vision. This subdivision would take my grandfather and his brother to a different level of business in the community. Many people would tell me that my grandfather sold them their first home.

As he continued to build his business platform, all his efforts to diversify the services he offered made him successful. He could imagine how he could take a vacant piece of land and make it into a vision and opportunity of a lifetime. From the developer of Teresa Terrace to contractor to real estate salesman, Americco would be known as the man to do business within Daly City.

A MAN OF MANY HATS

The Catholic hospital in San Francisco was overwhelmed with more than thirty thousand patients annually. An earthquake in 1957 that damaged the building led to a decision to build a new hospital. In 1965 a new hospital named Mary's Help Hospital was constructed in Daly City because northern San Mateo County needed a medical center and emergency room services.

My grandfather stepped in to be the real estate broker on behalf of the Catholic Hospital to buy the property for the new hospital site. Like its previous incarnations, it was designed to be a "sunshine hospital," meaning

Americco & Marie Lagomarsino

that every room had a windowed view so that natural sunlight could make it to the patients.

In addition to becoming the real estate broker for the Catholic hospital, my grandfather was one of the founding members of Mary's Help Hospital, aka Seton Hospital in Daly City. Being one of the founding fathers of Mary's Help Hospital was considered one of his most significant achievements by many who knew him.

Still, Americco had many vital contributions to the community and family. My grandfather wore many hats throughout his life, constantly finding new hats when new challenges presented themselves.

It could be overwhelming thinking about the many important jobs he had and how people entrusted him with their futures in every conceivable way. He was a natural leader with so much character and integrity; to be trusted by so many people is practically unheard of today.

FIRST NATIONAL BANK OF DALY CITY AND BEYOND

Another hat my grandfather wore was as the founder and chairman of the board of First National Bank of Daly City, a position he took after serving as Vice President of Systematic Savings & Loan in Daly City before its merger. Americco worked at the Savings

& Loan for over ten years, and during that time, many of his customers would ask him when he would start his bank. People in the community—my grandfather's customers at the Savings & Loan—trusted him with their life savings. These customers wanted a small local bank that served the community more than the big banks that were buying up the smaller banks.

My grandfather's approach was to be more intimate with his customers, how people today would describe their private banker. It seemed very natural to Americco to start a bank in the Daly City area. He asked various friends and business associates to invest and sit on the board of directors of First National Bank of Daly City, also known as First National Bank of Northern California.

The first bank building at 6600 Mission Street, Daly City, was completed on the third of May 1963. Before then, my grandfather had a temporary office for the bank at 150 San Pedro Road in Daly City until the new building's construction was completed on Mission Street. Americco was sixty years old when he started the bank in Daly City, and his project was considered his "baby," according to my mother. The community bank was the idea and brainchild of my grandfather. He felt it was his duty to make a success of the bank to his family and his investors.

I remember walking up to the new bank in Daly City, and the first thing I saw was the sparkles in the concrete on the sidewalk. Everything in the bank seemed to shine and sparkle like a jewel, just like my grandfather.

The bank was built in the modern style with concrete walls and tall ceilings as you entered the bank, along with white tile flooring and a large white teller counter space in the bank's interior. There was a massive steel bank vault in the back with large safety deposit boxes inside. Crystal chandeliers hung in the entrance, where there was a large sitting area for customers to wait. There was always coffee and cookies in the waiting area for the customers and lollipops for the children.

My grandfather continued to make improvements to the bank over the years. I still remember when he spearheaded getting a computer system in the bank in the 1960s, which was quite a massive undertaking at that time. Americco was so amazed when he talked about everything the computers would allow the bank to do.

All the banks had drive-up teller windows so that the customer need not get out of the car to make a transaction, Most families with children like the drive-up window because lollypops were always available for them.

Americco went on to build five additional banks before his death in 1972. The last bank to be created before my grandfather passed away was the Millbrae branch, but my grandfather didn't live long enough to see it open. In the end, my grandmother, Marie, would end up opening the Millbrae branch without Americco by her side. The Millbrae branch was my favorite bank because it was the last bank my grandfather had envisioned. All six banks Americco built had his framed portrait of himself hanging in the bank. I could always go into the bank and see his image on the wall.

Americco created a special "down to earth and home feeling" within his bank, and Americco wanted to "show real interest in the community and its residents and to serve local people." Americco decided the best way to serve local people was to find people *from* the community to serve on the board of directors of First National Bank of Daly City. Americco invited people with diverse occupations to be members.

The bank was chartered on the third of February 1963 by the following founding board of directors' members: T. Galt Atwood, Harry Carusis, Lawrence Vannucci, Gerald Mincher, Elton McGraw.

DEATH OF A BANKER

The day I learned my had grandfather died was just like any other spring afternoon living on Glen Avenue in San Bruno, other than the fact that my parents were not at home that day. I was eight years old, my birthday just a month away, and while I was outside playing, I noticed our neighbor had forgotten to pick up their newspaper. I decided to bring my neighbor her paper and knocked on the front door. When she opened the door, I handed her the newspaper, and she thanked me.

But then she said, "I'm sorry to hear about your grandfather's death."

I remember feeling shocked before blurting out, "No one told me my grandfather had passed away!" I walked back home in utter confusion about what my neighbor had just told me.

It turned out my grandfather had passed away the day before. My parents told us it was due to a massive heart attack, and he died at Mary's Help Hospital.

On the tenth of April 1972, Americco was rushed to Mary's Help Hospital complaining of severe abdominal pain. At the hospital, he had a massive heart attack and could not be revived.

My father told me that my grandfather knew the doctors had told him before that he needed heart surgery. Americco did not listen, and the only one who knew was my father, who was at the doctor's with my grandfather when the doctor told him he had a heart condition. No one in the family could understand what had happened to my grandfather. His wife Marie would be the one to find him in the living room, having terrible abdominal pain and heart problems. His death was an awful shock to all family members.

My grandfather's funeral would be one of the largest in the town of Colma. Everyone in the community came to honor him. My parents did not take me to the funeral, so I could never say goodbye to my grandfather.

Americco's best friend and attorney, Roe Ariani, would take my grandfather's place on the board of directors and as chairman of the board of First National Bank.

The news of my grandfather's death soon hit the local newspapers. According to the *San Mateo Times*, my grandfather would be interred at Olivetti Cemetery, where he and his family had worked. The Cemetery is near San Bruno Mountains, and is one of the oldest cemeteries in Colma.

My grandparents are in the mausoleums at Olivetti Cemetery along with William and Anna Lagomarsino—the four of them together in death as they were in life. Their headstones are on the same bottom row of the same mausoleum, not far from each other.

Also interred at Olivetti Cemetery is my mother, Louise Loretta Lagomarsino, who died at the age of fifty-four years old in September of 1992—the same age as my great-grandmother was when she passed away.

My grandfather was interred in the same cemetery his parents worked in when they came to America. He believed that his hometown was everything to him because it was where he was born. He was loyal to his city as he was with his family. The people in Colma and Daly City were like family to him, and he appreciated the life he created there.

THEN THERE WERE NONE

Herb Caen, a journalist for the *San Francisco Chronicle*, once interviewed my grandfather regarding the bank. The article's name was "Then There Was One," meaning one bank that had survived out of sixty other banks that started up in the 1960s. My grandfather's bank was the only one to make it.

Over the fifty-five years since its founding, my grandfather's bank has seen many competitor banks come and go. Some were bought out by larger banks, and others could not compete and closed up shop. The bank weathered many economic cycles and remained independent with banking decisions made locally. Americco never thought his empire would have grown to the extent it did over the last fifty-five years. Thinking about the odds he had to overcome to make his bank a success is hard to fathom in my mind.

In his interview with Herb Caen, my grandfather had noted that he believed people had the wrong idea about Daly City and that it was not acceptable to talk poorly about the city he loved so much. He said Daly City was more than just a town known for its gray and foggy weather, and no doubt he was thinking about the active community that he had helped develop with his housing development and bank.

It's true the bank soon became known as the "The Family Bank," and that image came from my grandfather, who designed the logo of the family set in stone at the front entrance of the Daly City branch. The treatment of consumer and business clients like family is still going strong today. During the past fifty-five years of deliberate and steady growth, that "family bank" feel has never been lost. Though banking has changed a lot in the years since my grandfather started the bank, what remained the same is that the branch managers listen to their customers.

Another significant change has been that the bank has grown from one branch with one million dollars in assets to twelve branches, eight in San Mateo County, one branch in Santa Clara and three in San Francisco, and over six hundred million dollars in assets. In 1995, given the bank's geographic diversity, the board of directors voted to change the bank's name to the First National Bank of Northern California.

At one time, the stock was bought by private investors of the bank only. For the first time, the First National Bank of Northern California was sold on the NASDAQ. My grandfather could never have imagined how his bank would have survived for fifty-five years.

Our family interest in the bank remained secure, between the stockholdings we continued to hold in First National Bank of Northern California and Americco's family attorney Roe Ariani taking his place as chairman of the board of directors. Roe Ariani did a great job representing our family's interest in the bank, and it continued to grow under his direction. When Roe Ariani passed away about twenty years ago, my older sister sat on the board of directors of the bank. It was during this time the board decided to sell the bank.

First National Bank of Northern California had been looking for another bank to acquire their assets for a while. My mother told me before she passed away in 1992 that the bank would sell one day. Although she thought the bank would be sold within five or ten years from her death, little did she know that it would take over twenty-five years for the bank to be acquired.

The board of directors and shareholders were all in agreement that they were considering offers by another bank. In the end, it was Tri-County Bank and its parent company, TriCo Bancshares, that acquired First National Bank of Northern California in July of 2018, in a stock transaction valued at approximately 315.3 million dollars.

TriCo became one of the largest, if not the largest, community banks in Northern California. The partnership was a good fit since TriCo was active in home and construction loans, similar to First National Bank of Northern California.

Americco's stockholding in First National Bank of Northern California pretty much guaranteed that our family would remain on the board of directors for the lifetime of the bank. But with the sale of the bank to TriCo, we would no longer hold a position on the board. Even so, I know my grandfather would have felt optimistic about the sale of the bank to another community bank in Northern California.

The reputation of the town of Daly City was crucial to Americco, and he just thought it was the best place on earth to live. He took a lot of pride in being a member of the community in Daly City and making a difference for a better life for everyone he served. The family was important to him, and he always wanted people to treat customers like family—something the new owners of the bank say they will continue.

I have always believed that my grandfather was the type of person who wanted to lift people up and not bring them down. Like a cheerleader cheering for the team, Americco was always a team player and a leader. I think he might have looked at the sale of the bank regarding whether it was good for everybody. Never did he feel about just himself to get ahead in life. It was always about family, and that's why the bank was called and known as "The Family Bank," and it's why I hope the bank will continue to uphold the values and traditions that my grandfather Americco started in 1963.

NONI MARIE'S ITALIAN RECIPES

RICE TORTA

4 - 5 cups of cooked rice

1 cup of breadcrumbs

1 cup Parmesan cheese

1 cup Monterey Jack cheese

½ cup chopped basil

¼ cup olive oil

1 chopped onion

4 chopped cloves garlic

1 tbsp Italian seasoning

1 tbsp salt & pepper

2 - 3 eggs

Preheat oven to 350 degrees F. Take a metal pan 9-inch x 13-inch and coat lightly with olive oil. Add breadcrumbs to the pan, coating the bottom and sides with breadcrumbs. Take 4 cups of cooked rice in a large bowl, mix in both kinds of cheese, chopped onion, garlic, basil, Italian seasoning, olive oil, salt, and pepper in a bowl.

Add 2 to 3 eggs in the mix and stir together until completely mixed. Add to metal pan and spread mixture evenly over pan and bake for 35 to 45 minutes or until top is brown. Take out of the oven and cool and cut into 3-inch x 3-inch squares. Can be eaten hot or cold; refrigerate after cooking. Enjoy!

ITALIAN STUFFED ZUCCHINI

6 large zucchinis

½ - 1 lb cooked chopped Italian sausage

1 cup Parmesan cheese

1 cup Monterey Jack cheese

½ cup chopped basil

1 chopped onion

4 cloves chopped garlic

1 tbsp Italian seasoning

1 tbsp salt & pepper

2 - 3 eggs

Preheat oven to 350 degrees. Take a metal pan 9-inch x 13-inch and coat lightly with olive oil. Boil zucchini until able to cut in half easily. Hollow out zucchini to make them into shells. Take the zucchini pieces and put them into a large bowl to strain the water from the remaining zucchini.

In the same large bowl, after straining, mix in both kinds of cheese, cooked and chopped Italian sausage, chopped onion, garlic, basil, Italian seasoning, salt, and pepper in a bowl. Add 2 to 3 eggs in the mix and stir together until completely mixed.

Add mixture to zucchini shells and spread mixture evenly over shells, then bake for 35 to 45 minutes or until top is brown. Take out of the oven and cool. Can be eaten hot or cold; refrigerate after cooking. Enjoy!

ZUCCHINI AND SPINACH FRITTATA

2 cups chopped spinach
2 cups chopped zucchini
1 cup Parmesan cheese
1 cup Monterey Jack cheese
½ cup chopped basil
1 chopped onion
4 cloves chopped garlic
1 tbsp Italian seasoning
1 tbsp salt & pepper
2 - 3 eggs

Preheat oven to 350 degrees and bake for 35 to 45 mins or until top is brown. Take a metal pan 9-inch x 13-inch and coat lightly with olive oil. Boil zucchini and spinach until tender. In a large bowl, strain excess water from the zucchini and spinach.

After straining, in the same large bowl, mix in both kinds of cheese, chopped onion, garlic, basil, Italian seasoning, salt, and pepper in a bowl. Add 2 to 3 eggs in the mix and stir together until completely mixed. Add mixture to the pan, spread evenly over the baking pan, and bake for 35 to 45 minutes. Take out of the oven and cool. Can be eaten hot or cold; refrigerate after cooking. Enjoy!

Italian Spinach Stuffing For Turkey

1 loaf of bread (any kind)
½ cup butter (salted or unsalted)
1 cup Parmesan cheese
½ cup chopped basil
1 chopped onion
4 cloves chopped garlic
1 tbsp Italian seasonings
1 tbsp salt & pepper
2 - 3 eggs

Melt ½ cup of butter in a large saucepan on medium heat on the stove. Once melted, tear bread into pieces and drop into the butter, toasting until brown (wet bread with a little bit of water if that makes it easier to tear into pieces). Stir mixture in pan and add onion and garlic. Cook until fragrant and the whole loaf of bread has been turned into small, golden-brown bread balls.

Take the cooked mixture and in a large bowl, mix breadcrumbs and cheese, basil, Italian seasoning, salt, and pepper in a bowl. Add 2 to 3 eggs in the mix and stir together until completely mixed. Add mixture to the stuffed turkey. Bake for 35 to 45 minutes or until the turkey reaches an internal temperature of 165 degrees F. Take out of the oven and cool. Enjoy!

ABOUT THE AUTHOR

Jacqueline L. Foster was born on the tenth of May 1963, one week after the new First National Bank of Daly City opened on Mission Street. The founding of the bank marks her birth.

She has lived in the San Francisco Bay Area most all her life. She has been a Certified Residential Real Estate Appraiser since 2001 and has constructed and designed two custom single-family residential homes in San Mateo County. Currently, Foster is working on her bachelor's degree in Criminal Justice.

Today, she lives in the Silicon Valley area with her daughter and her grandson. Spending over two years researching her grandfather's history from public records and census information has given her the chance to find out information she had never known about her family. This experience has been truly fascinating for her to explore the life story of her grandfather.

It's difficult to remember every detail of her grandfather at a young age, but she still has memories of her grandfather that she recalls to this day. That's how big of an impact Americco had on her life.

To all the family members who said she could never write a book? The cemetery owners told her grandfather he would never be successful in business; just like her grandfather, she likes to prove people wrong.

ENDNOTES

CHAPTER 1

Ancestry.com The United States. Department of Commerce: Census Bureau. Decennial Census:1910, 1920, 1930,1940, 1950, 1960, 1970. Washington, D.C.: GPO.

Gillespie, Bunny. *Images of America: Daly City*. Charleston: Arcadia Publisher, 2003, 46,71,102.

Gillespie, Bunny, and Crimmen, Dave. *Then & Now Daly City*. Charleston: Arcadia Publishing, 2011, 101.

Smookler, Michael. *Images of America: San Mateo County Coast*. Charleston: Arcadia Publishing, 2007, 38, 48, 55-56.

Cavour Camillo *Italian Unification* https://en.wikipedia.org/wiki/Italian_unification

1906 San Francisco earthquake https://en.wikipedia.org/wiki/1906_San_Francisco_earthquake

CHAPTER 2

Holy Cross Cemetery Colma, California dated March 2018

https://en.wikipedia.org/wiki/Holy_Cross_Cemetery_(Colma%2C_California)

Asbury, Herbert: *The Barbary Coast*: An Informal History of the San Francisco Underworld. New York: Basic Books, 2002 Pg. 104.

CHAPTER 3

Tealdi, Elia: *Eulogy & Obituary*, date February 2005

HMS Princess Irene https://en.wikipedia.org/wiki/HMS_Princess_Irene

Ancestry.com The United States. Department of Commerce: Census Bureau. Decennial Census:1910, 1920, 1930,1940, 1950, 1960, 1970. Washington, D.C.: GPO.

CHAPTER 4

Saints Peter and Paul Catholic Church, San Francisco, California https://en.wikipedia.org/wiki/Saints_Peter_and_Paul_Church,_San_Francisco

CHAPTER 8

Seton Hospital aka Mary's Help Hospital, Daly City, California https://en.wikipedia.org/wiki/Seton_Hospital_Daly_City_CA

"Death Claims Civic Leader Lagomarsino." *The Times*, 10 April 1972, p. 40.

CHAPTER 9

Cynthia. Sweeney. "TriCo acquires First National Bank of Northern California." *The North Bay Business Journal*, 12 December 2017. Retrieved from https://www.businesswire.com/news/home/20171211006325/en/TriCo-Bancshares-Enters-San-Francisco-Bay-Area.

Chapter 11

Bartlett, Jean. "The journey of Daly City 'adopted son' Tom McGraw of First National Bank." *The Mercury News*, 8 May 2012.

Caen, Herb. "Then There Was One." *San Francisco Chronicle*, 1970, p. 14.

TRUST FUND
BABY

PROLOGUE
"YOU'RE NOT GOING TO SHOOT MY MOTHER!"

As I creep up the stairs, my father's shouts become louder, along with my mother's sobs. On this particular Sunday in 1972, my half-sisters are out of the house with their father for the afternoon, so there's no one to stop nine-year-old me from investigating the commotion.

I pause at the door to their bedroom and peek inside. My mother kneels on the floor while my father looms over her, holding a gun to her head. Fury is splashed across his face. For a moment, I freeze. Do I scream? Run away? Watch helplessly as my father fires the gun?

My indecision doesn't last long. I fling open the door and rush into my shocked mother's arms. I scream at my father, "You're not going to shoot my mother!" He stares at me in stunned silence, mouth agape.

My mother seizes the opportunity. She yanks me out of the room, and together, we run down the stairs. She stops only to grab her purse before throwing me into her car and putting the pedal to the metal. As we drive, I begin to understand what true fear is.

The most traumatic incident of my childhood left its mark in my aversion to guns and abhorrence of violence. However, it was also the moment that set me on the path to breaking my family's cycle of physical and emotional abuse.

It would not be the last time I witnessed—and experienced—violence in my family. My mother returned to my father, and his abuse escalated in the ensuing years. My half-sisters followed in his footsteps, and their cruelty became a defining feature in my life.

However, I was blessed with the love of my mother and her father, the most wonderful grandfather in the world. Guided by their examples, I did not stoop to my family's level. Instead, I emerged from my childhood with a commitment to fight injustice—first, as my mother's protector and voice, and later, by fighting against my family's mismanagement of my grandfather's inheritance.

I do not wish the experiences recounted in this book on my worst enemy. However, by telling my story, I prove to myself and those who have tried to silence my voice for nearly six decades that I am a survivor—not a victim—of their abuse. If my life can show another survivor a path to overcome their own fear and pain without resorting to violence, substance abuse, or destructive habits, something positive will have come out of something terrible. I couldn't ask for a greater purpose than that.

YOUR LIFE HAS BEEN PLANNED BEFORE YOUR BIRTH

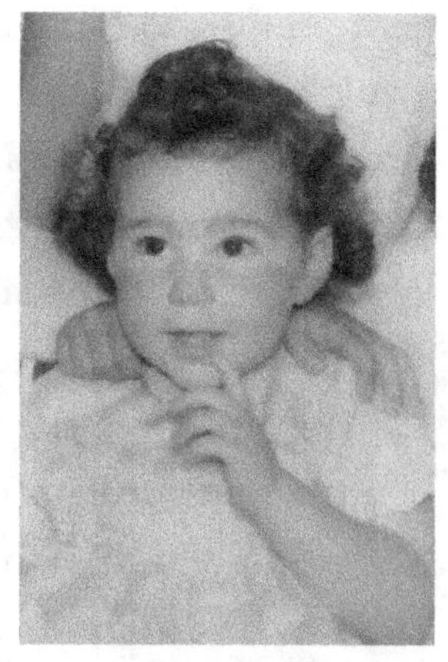

My family's cycle of violence began long before I showed up. My mother, Louise Loretta Lagomarsino, grew up with two loving parents and a sister in Daly City, just outside of San Francisco. However, when she found herself pregnant at eighteen, she married her high school sweetheart. They went on to have three daughters together: Liza and, later, twins Laurel and Linda.

My mother's life with Rhonny Angelost was nothing like the family she grew up in. He was physically and emotionally abusive, and he belittled her constantly. When he was upset, he had a habit of throwing the dinner she prepared for him onto the floor. His behavior crossed the line from cruelty into life-threatening: he once refused to drive her to the hospital when she was suffering from blood poisoning. Nevertheless, my mother stuck by him; divorce was unheard of in her traditional Italian Catholic family.

Rhonny did not confine his abuse to my mother. Liza revealed that her father had molested her and her sisters when she was five. I can only imagine the horror my mother must have felt when she realized what had happened. That was the last straw: she gathered her courage and left Rhonny for good.

Some time later, a friend set my mother up on a blind date with Jon Foster, a construction contractor and truck driver. He had spent time in juvenile hall, was functionally illiterate because of severe dyslexia, and had a Napoleon complex. Yet, she must have seen something in him—he became my father. When she was pregnant with me, she had a decision to make. Despite everything that had passed between them, Rhonny desperately wanted her to return to him and promised he would raise me as one of his own children. Fortunately, my mother knew better. In no uncertain terms, she told him, "You already molested three of my children, and you're not getting another. I ain't going back to you." With that, she committed to raising her family with Jon. They married and settled nearby her parents in Daly City.

My birth was the next dramatic chapter in my family's saga. It turned out my mother developed a bad habit of marrying men who refused to drive her to the hospital: when she went into labor on May 10, 1963, my father wouldn't budge from the house until he had taken a shower. His selfishness cost precious time. Shortly after they hopped in the car, I came into the world. However, I was not out of the woods yet: my face was blue from the umbilical cord wrapped around my neck. To his credit, my father remained calm. Without stopping the car, he unwound the umbilical cord, and I took my first breath.

I had never shaken the feeling that I had died before I was even born. My near-death experience mirrors those of many others who have come back from the other side more empathetic to the things that cannot be seen. This empathy has guided me on my journey to understand why I was put on this earth. Everyone has a mission to fulfill before their time is done. I instinctively fought hard to come into the world, but it would be many years before I understood why.

❧

My parents named me Jacqueline Loretta after two strong, beautiful women: Jacqueline, for then-First Lady Jacqueline Kennedy, and Loretta, after my mother.

As a child, I was the smallest one in my family and had a head full of curly red hair. As I grew older, my hair darkened into brown, but I remained petite and always looked younger than I was—a trait I have since come to appreciate. Unlike my half-sisters, I never gave my mother cause for concern: I was shy, quiet, and devoutly religious. More of a lover than a fighter, I avoided conflict like the plague.

At school, I was known as "Little Jackie Foster." A learning disability made reading, spelling, and writing challenging, and I struggled with my schoolwork. Nevertheless, I was never in trouble, which was just as well—I had enough of it at home.

Growing up, I often felt like Cinderella. However, she only had two evil stepsisters to worry about—I had three scary half-sisters. I should have known what I was in for when shortly after my birth, they demanded my mother take me back to the hospital. From the beginning, the differences between us were stark.

Liza, my oldest sister, was born six years before I was. As my mother's first child and the family's first grandchild, she was as bossy and spoiled as could be expected. She frequently crossed the line into bullying, and when we bickered, she would sit on me until I surrendered. Moreover, her penchant for saying the wrong thing at the wrong time did not endear her to her classmates or me. My half-sisters and I once had to transfer schools because Liza ran her mouth off to her classmates. She frequently shoplifted despite my parents and grandparents handing her everything on a silver platter. Even as a child, she rarely laughed or smiled, and as she grew older, she never developed a sense of humor.

Liza may not have inherited a funny bone, but everything was a joke to my twin sisters Laurel and Linda. The "terrible twins," as my exasperated mother called them, were as devious as children come. They were known to clog the toilet with bathroom tissue and make mayonnaise and mustard sandwiches—on the couch in the living room. They didn't behave any better in public. At the grocery store, they would purposefully run off in opposite directions, forcing my mother and Liza to split up to chase after them. Laurel was cold and distant and, as we grew older, frequently jealous of me. Linda was sly but also very anxious. I remember her hands constantly shaking.

Their father's abuse was no doubt to blame for much of their rambunctious behavior. Nevertheless, the twins crossed the line from harmless prank into cruelty when it came to me. One day when I was four years old, they were playing in our home's driveway with the iron gate in front of the house wide open. As younger sisters do, I toddled along after them, eager to join in their games.

When Laurel and Linda saw me, they shared a look and spoke in a language only they understood. Before I realized what was happened, they ran towards the house and slammed the gate shut behind them, leaving me stranded on the outside. Separated from my family by what seemed at the time to be the tallest gate in the world, I did the only thing I could think of: I started to climb.

Big mistake. As I neared the top, the twins swung the gate open, and I dropped to the concrete below with a thud. I screamed. My mother ran down the front steps with her hands to her face, screaming along with me. She picked me up and brought me inside to my bedroom. Once there, she slapped a Band-Aid on my leg and, in her most soothing tone, promised I would be just fine.

However, there are some things not even a mother's love can heal. When I still couldn't walk several days later, it was clear that the fall had broken my leg. My parents took me to the hospital. This time, my father already had plenty of opportunities to take a shower. Fortunately, there was no lasting damage—physically, anyway.

To this day, my strongest memory of that day is the peals of my half-sisters' laughter. That was when I realized there was something horribly wrong with my family.

BLOOD IS THICKER THAN MONEY

I grew up steeped in family history, literally. We lived in a subdivision in Daly City called Teresa Terrace, a development named for my great-grandmother and developed by my grandfather, Americco Lagomarsino. The son of Italian immigrants, he was primarily raised by his long-suffering mother, Teresa Lagomarsino. Her husband was unfaithful and eventually left her with four sons to raise—and a fatal case of syphilis.

With a gleam in his eye, my grandfather would always say, "It's one thing to make money; it's another to keep it!" However, he figured out the secret. Despite having only an eighth-grade education, my grandfather transformed himself from a laborer into an insurance salesman, a general contractor, a real estate businessman, and eventually, the founder of the First National Bank of Daly City.

After he left school, my grandfather worked with his brothers in a cemetery by day. By night, they sold just about every kind of insurance door to door. When he was thirty-five, he and his brother William risked everything and left their steady jobs to start their own insurance company. On the day he quit his day job, his employer told him, "You will never be successful in business in your life."

He could not have been more wrong. William Lagomarsino & Company soon expanded well beyond insurance. My grandfather became a general contractor and real estate broker, and with these skills, he built homes on a property he named Teresa Terrace. He and his brother then invested their profits in other properties. Eventually, his success led him to found the First National Bank of Daly City, later known as First National Bank of Northern California. It opened exactly one week before I was born—a sign of how close we would become.

My grandfather worked tirelessly to provide his wife, Marie Tealdi, and his two daughters—my mother, Louise, and my aunt, Diva—the material comforts he never had. I remember the house he and my grandmother built together as being filled with love and laughter throughout my childhood.

Despite his difficult upbringing and the challenges that came along with his success, not once did I ever see my grandfather raise his voice in anger. He always had a smile on his face, especially when he saw his grandchildren. My half-sisters, cousins, and I spent many happy hours at my grandparents' house. Every day when he finished work, my grandfather would open the door between the downstairs office and the upstairs apartment, and we grandchildren would run down the long hallway. He would open his arms wide, grab all of us at the same time, and carry us down the hall to his big chair in the living room. There, we would gather around as he told us stories.

His calm, upbeat demeanor could not have been more different from that of my father and half-sisters. For that alone, I adored and admired him. The feeling was very much mutual.

One Easter, he took our family out to eat at Nick's Rockaway. I remember it had a beautiful view of the Pacific Ocean. I stood at the end of the parking lot by a seawall, leaning over to glimpse the beach below. Just then, a gust of wind blew my little bow from my hair onto the sand. Without hesitation, my grandfather ran down onto the beach, picked up my bow, and brought it back to me with a grin. That was the kind of person he was: he would do anything to make the people he loved happy.

By the time he died of a heart attack on April 10, 1972, he and his brother jointly owned approximately one hundred properties. His financial success changed my life and the lives of my relatives forever. His death made me, at eight years old, a two-percenter: part of the two percent of people who have trust funds. Not that anyone would have known it—I grew up in a middle-class neighborhood in a middle-class town, and that did not change after his death. Still, our modest lifestyle did not stop my mother from worrying about my half-sisters and me being kidnapped and held for ransom. I don't know who would have wanted the four of us; they would have sent us back real quick.

After my grandfather died, in addition to his wealth, my mother and aunt inherited the responsibility and pressure of dividing up the brothers' properties, settling his estate, choosing which properties to keep and which to sell, paying estate taxes, and managing the trust fund his will established. Overnight, my mother, a housewife, had to become a businesswoman. Fortunately, she had a knack for it, just like her father. My aunt, an interior decorator by training, did not. As a result, she put enormous strain on my mother.

My grandfather was the glue that held all of us together, and nothing was ever the same again. When he died, it was inevitable that greed would poison our relationships and eventually tear our family apart. More cracks started to show two years later, in 1974, when my grandmother died. Like my grandfather, her will left equal portions of her estate to each grandchild, with larger shares for my mother and aunt. Her will also established a trust fund. Each of us was to receive an annual income from the trust.

This was not enough money to satisfy my aunt. She insisted the estate be split down the middle and divided between her and my mother so that down the line, her two children would inherit more than me and my three half-sisters. As the executor of the estate, my mother was torn between her mother's final wishes and her sister's demands.

One day in the midst of this dispute, my aunt showed up at our house armed with a hammer. She walked into our garage and began swinging the hammer and destroying a large ceramic sculpture. It was only much later that I understood the cause of her bizarre behavior and learned that I was supposed to have inherited another trust fund.

The strain my aunt put on my mother was enormous, and eventually, for the sake of their relationship, my mother agreed to destroy my grandmother's will. The estate went through probate court and was divided in half. My aunt had won—and my mother had lost—in every way. Despite everything she did to keep the peace, my mother's relationship with her sister barely survived the ordeal. It was a sign of things to come.

FAMILY STRIFE

My family's financial position was the only aspect of my childhood that was secure. The day I was born was the day my half-sisters found a lifelong scapegoat for every unpleasant aspect of their lives.

Despite their father's abuse, Liza, Laurel, and Linda blamed me for their parents' divorce. Rhonny resented our mother for not taking him back, and whenever he saw his daughters, he whispered poison in their ears. "You're better than she is," he would say. "She's not one of us." My half-sisters took his words to heart and never let me forget it. They did everything they could to remind me throughout my childhood that because I wasn't an Angelost, I was the odd one out in the family.

In retrospect, that was something to be grateful for. The first time I met Rhonny, I was four years old. He asked me if I wanted candy, and like any kid, I said yes. I couldn't reach the candy on the top shelf, so Rhonny lifted me up to it. As he did, he stuck his hand under my dress. Even then, I knew his behavior was wrong. The second time, I was ten years old. Linda had begged me to come to his house with her, and while we were playing in a bedroom, he walked in, sat in a chair, and stared at me intently. I couldn't shake the feeling he was undressing me with his eyes and was terrified of what he might do. I never went back.

In many ways, my half-sisters took after Rhonny; their physical abuse started early. Just like their father did to them, both Liza and Linda molested me as a baby and a small child. Liza treated me as her "dolly," while Linda insisted on playing doctor with me. When I was older, Liza, who was always heavyset, would sit on me as I was lying in bed and trap me as she put on her shoes. I fought back as best I could; despite being so small, I was the perfect height to hit her on her butt.

The emotional abuse was just as cruel. My half-sisters constantly belittled me. Among other names, they called me "stupid" because of my learning disability. Laurel and Linda did not learn their lesson about tricks after they broke my leg: I vividly remember them putting clay in my bed and telling me it was cat poop. They made it so I never felt safe, physically or emotionally, in my own home.

I stood apart from my half-sisters in ways besides my last name. Unlike them, I inherited all the genes for athletics; they could not catch a ball if their lives depended on it. I played sports throughout school, loved dancing, and even became an aerobics instructor. In fifth and seventh grade, I made the cheerleading squad. I beamed with pride when I put on my uniform. However, Laurel's jealousy quickly wiped the smile right off my face. She tried and failed to make the team and refused to speak to me whenever I wore the uniform. That resentment persisted throughout our school years even though she was a straight-A student. I looked up to all of my big sisters as a child, but whenever my eyes met Laurel's, I could feel her hatred.

As I entered adolescence, my half-sisters tormented me with constant criticism. They would get upset if I put on even one swipe of mascara. I never dressed provocatively, but that didn't stop them from insisting I put on more clothes—even if I was wearing a tube top with a shirt underneath! I understand now that much of their anger came from envy. I was the only one of us who had cleavage, and they likely suffered from body dysmorphic disorder. Linda steadfastly refused to show any part of her body outside the house, while Laurel, who had scoliosis, had both breast implants and plastic surgery.

I was not the only one who had a difficult relationship with my half-sisters. They often fought bitterly, and sometimes, physically, with my father, Jon Foster. On occasion, they made false accusations about his mistreatment of them and would consistently tell me how much they despised not only him but our mother as well. They never forgave her for leaving their father. Still, as we grew older, none of that stopped my half-sisters from befriending my father, earning his trust, and using it to turn him against me. In later years, Laurel grew so close to him that he sold her cocaine—her drug of choice—while helping her care for her dying husband. Throughout my childhood and into adulthood, they would manipulate him to make me and my mother miserable and punish us for their unhappiness.

My half-sisters filled my childhood with abuse, gaslighting, and terror. I would lie awake at night praying that God would stop the abuse and help me understand why they hated me. Because of their animosity, I never knew what it was like to have the support of a loving family. It was no wonder I developed a Cinderella complex. For many years, I clung to the need to be taken care of. It seemed like an eternity before my prince arrived.

My half-sisters were far from the only nightmares of my childhood. I had been afraid of my father ever since I walked in on him threatening my mother with a gun. He was violent towards my mother, Liza, and Linda, and sometimes, their fist-fights would end with knockout punches. Even at the age of twelve, I knew better than to complain when he would force me to wash his truck and drive with him while he was hauling dirt to read the maps and street signs.

My father's favorite punishment was humiliation. When he felt my half-sisters and I had misbehaved, he would force us to line up and hit us with his belt, one by one. Other times, he would take us over his knee and spank us in front of everyone. By the time I was sixteen, I had my own car and a job in sales and finance at a department store. None of that mattered; he would still find excuses to hit me. I realize now how much of his behavior was driven by his need to control our family. The older I got, the more my fear grew, and I knew I had to escape, one way or another.

My mother was the only one of my family members who ever asked how I was or offered me help and support. She spoiled me with love instead of things. Thanks to her, our rooms were always tidy, and there was a fresh-cooked meal on the dinner table every night.

She took care of everyone in our family—even her "fifth child." After my grandfather died, my father mostly stopped working. My mother bought him everything he wanted, and instead of contributing to the family by helping around the house, he spent his days sitting around and smoking pot. The only loving fatherly advice he ever gave me was: "I've tried every drug in the world, and they were all no good, so you don't need to try them."

Fortunately, I took his words to heart and was one of the few in my family who avoided the pitfalls of drug and alcohol abuse.

Regardless, my mother bore her burdens without complaint and was the best parent I could have asked for. However, all of that changed when I was sixteen. Instead of running around the house taking care of my half-sisters and me, I would come home from school to find her drunk on the couch, spouting off conspiracy theories and talking nonsense. The pressure of an abusive husband, difficult daughters, a greedy sister, and her responsibilities as a financial steward pushed her beyond her limits, and she had a nervous breakdown. She was involuntarily committed to a hospital, where she remained for three weeks. The doctors diagnosed her with bipolar disorder and prescribed her lithium. All of a sudden, I had to grow up real fast.

And when it rains, it pours. Shortly after she returned home, it was my father's turn to have a breakdown. He, too, was hospitalized. Their marriage ended not long after his release. No surprise, my sisters added the breakup to their long list of crimes I was responsible for.

Even though my mother was the breadwinner, my father kicked her out of the family home. I was desperate to live with her. However, he was a master manipulator and insisted I stay with him—not out of love, respect, or concern for me, but simply so he could collect alimony and child support.

As difficult as my home life was before, it became intolerable. I needed to get out. Fortunately, fate stepped in. I was cruising down the famous street El Camino one day when I was seventeen, and I spotted Bill Rivers. He had muscles on top of muscles and the greenest eyes I had ever seen. We pulled over in our cars, talked for a while, and exchanged numbers. That was it.

He became my big teddy bear, and for the first time, I felt safe. One day, he showed up at my house, helped me load my things into the back of his truck, and together, we drove off into the sunset. I never lived under my father's roof again.

Bill and I were condo owners before our twentieth birthdays. We married on December 23, 1984, in Lake Tahoe, Nevada, when I was twenty-one. Although we later divorced, in those early years, we adored each other. In 1987, we had a beautiful daughter together. Finally, after years of abuse, humiliation, and fear, I created a family that had not pain but love at its center.

DON'T LET ANYONE DESTROY YOUR SPIRIT

Real estate was in my blood, so it was only fitting that I would follow in my grandfather's footsteps as I began my own career. While working as an excavation contractor on a job site, Bill came across a piece of land in Pescadero, California, and saw something special in it. We bought it for $30,000 and built our first custom-designed house in the same year our daughter was born. The experience was exhilarating.

The year 1987 was good to us. We started a successful excavation business with dump trucks and tractors. Between digging septic tanks and digging foundations, Bill knew more about construction than anyone I had ever met except for my grandfather. I like to think he would have approved of my marriage. Like my grandfather, Bill was a savvy businessman with a talent for making money. He would work all day at his construction job and then come home to make phone calls all night—and he did it all with a smile on his face. Perhaps it was that quality that attracted me to him. Just like my grandfather, everybody who knew Bill loved him.

I began the next chapter in my professional life in 1990. My mother came to me with the idea to start our own company to manage the trust fund-owned properties we inherited from my grandfather. She didn't have to ask me twice. Ever the peacemaker, she had already invited Liza and Laurel to join her in the new venture. Their reaction was not encouraging.

They were livid and threatened to break the trust if she took over the management of our family's properties. Nevertheless, she did not give in to their pressure, and we opened Lagomarsino Properties Management. Liza and Laurel ridiculed us, called us crazy, and harassed us. When none of that did any good, they broke off most communication. Their lowest blow came when they hired an attorney to document all our office's conflicts of interest and send our mother a letter detailing each and every one, no matter how small. My mother didn't have a malicious bone in her body; every mistake she made was due to her lack of formal training as a property manager. Her only crime, at least in this family, was trying to do a good thing for us. My half-sisters' hostility was devastating to her, and my heart ached to see her suffer. Nevertheless, I supported her and our business as best I could. After starting classes in 1991, I earned my real estate license in 1994.

It did not help that my half-sisters grew closer to our Aunt Diva in these years and frequently took her side in family disagreements. They behaved as if they were her daughters instead of our mother's. As the rift in the family widened, childhood patterns repeated themselves, and I bore the brunt of Liza and Laurel's anger. Holidays together were more stressful than they were worth. Laurel, in particular, made clear her distaste for my daughter and me. My half-sisters shunned me and refused to invite me to family events, including our mother's fiftieth birthday party. Their cruelty and pettiness cut just as deeply as they did then.

❧

In 1992, after returning from a trip to Disneyland, my mother found a lump on the back of her neck. Her test results gave us the worst possible news: she had lung cancer and had less than six months to live. After her diagnosis, Liza and Laurel came back into the family fold and immediately resumed their bullying. Without anyone's permission, Liza took over our mother's health care, her financial and legal responsibilities, and just about everything else. I suppose I should have been grateful that she "allowed" me to continue managing the Lagomarsino Properties Management business.

Before the prodigal daughters returned, my mother had confided in me that she was leaving her entire estate to Linda and me, with nothing for Liza and Laurel. However, when Liza found out, she wouldn't stand for it. As my mother was on her deathbed, she browbeat her into firing her own lawyer and using Liza's to rewrite her will. The new version divided her estate equally between my half-sisters and me, with an inheritance for my father and my mother's boyfriend.

My mother, the one member of my immediate family who loved and cared about me, died in September 1992 at the age of fifty-four. I was only twenty-nine years old and heartbroken. However, I appeared to be the only one. Liza and I were executors of her estate, and as usual, she railroaded me at every turn. She insisted we clear out my mother's house and divvy up her belongings almost immediately. It didn't matter that I was nowhere near ready to begin that process. Because we owed significant inheritance taxes, we had to sell several properties. One of these was my mother's condo in Lake Tahoe. It had been her wish that it stay in the family, but my half-sisters were adamant that we sell it. I could see clear as day that it was pointless trying to keep the four of us together.

Despite my experience in real estate, my half-sisters refused to allow me to be the agent for the properties, claiming it was a conflict of interest—a term they threw around when it conveniently benefited them and wounded me. It pained me not to be able to use the skillset I worked hard to develop for the benefit of my mother's estate. The real estate agent they hired ultimately sold ten of my mother's properties below market value, and it took us ten years to pay off the taxes.

DON'T LET ANYONE
DEFINE YOU

"Listen," I say, trying not to raise my voice. "I'm not taking care of you. You never took care of me, my mother, or my half-sisters. Why should I spend my life taking care of you?" Before she died, my mother told me she left money to my father purposefully so I wouldn't have to shoulder the burden of caring for him. I look him in the eye. "I won't do it."

Anger flashes across my father's face. My stomach drops. It's a look I've seen before. He grabs a gun and points it at my head. "I brought you into this world, and I'm going to take you out of it." The most traumatic moment of my childhood is repeating itself. Except this time, I'm the one with the gun to her head.

Somehow, I find the strength to throw my five-year-old daughter in the closet and shut the door. I may not be able to protect myself, but I can at least protect her from the sight of her grandfather murdering her mother. Then, I beg the way my mother must've twenty years before. "Please don't shoot me in front of my kid."

It feels like an eternity before he laughs and lowers the gun. "There aren't any bullets in it."

I don't wait around for him to load it. I grab my daughter and run out of there faster than I ever have before.

By the time the police arrived at my condo in Burlingame, California, my father was gone—along with his guns and half of my belongings. He was always stealing from someone, so I should not have been surprised. Nor should I have been surprised by my half-sisters' reaction to the incident: "Stop being so dramatic," they said. "You're making it up!" They told me and anyone who would listen that I was crazy and worthless.

I only saw my father twice in the nearly thirty years after that. Once, I spotted him in a car while I was driving. I stuck my head out the window and shouted, "Jon, remember me? I'm your daughter!" Did he pull over? Did he wave? Did he even smile? Of course not. He simply shook his head and kept driving.

The other time, I was picking up my grandson from daycare when I saw him get off a bus. I chased him down the street. "Jon! Jon!" I shouted. He kept walking until he reached a train track. I caught up with him, and he had no choice but to listen to me. "Look, Jon, it's me, Jackie, your daughter."

His only reply was, "I wouldn't have recognized you."

I kept trying. "Do you want to meet your great-grandson?"

"No, I don't want to see him."

There was nothing else to say. I shrugged. "Okay, Jon. Take care of yourself." I turned around and walked away.

In that moment, I realized the years had cooled my anger, and I bore him no ill will. I never saw him again. I did not learn until much later that he had passed away in June 2015 at the age of seventy-eight.

In the years after my mother's death, I was in touch with Liza, Laurel, and Linda only sporadically. When they weren't refusing to acknowledge my daughter and me, they were telling me how much everyone in our family hated my guts. Before she died, my mother had warned me that they had it in for me. It hurt to hear, but her words validated my intuition. I had already been pulling away from them for years, but after another four years of struggling, it was my turn to shun them.

I separated myself from them completely, and the feeling was mutual—they wanted nothing to do with me, either. For the first time in my life, I was free to focus entirely on my own well-being and that of my daughter.

I set about building a network of people who would lift me up in the way my blood relatives never had. That was easier said than done. After surviving an abusive childhood, I was confident I would never again be a victim of domestic violence. However, I learned the hard way to never say never—once abused, always abused. Those of us who have endured those experiences must be vigilant about falling back into those relationships for the rest of our lives.

My personality didn't help. I am empathetic to a fault and will give someone the shirt off my back. But unfortunately, that makes me vulnerable to falling for those who would take advantage of me. A therapist once called me "Doris the Doormat," and I lived up to the name for many years.

It was a bittersweet thing to be in my financial position. I never knew if someone liked me for who I was or for my money, and time and time again, I fell into the trap of being someone's meal ticket. I would have traded my entire trust fund for a family that cared about me.

❧

Even in the early 1990s, when I was studying to become a certified real estate agent, I wanted to become an appraiser. Those were the days immediately following the savings and loan crisis, and California was just beginning to license appraisers. I used to poke my head into those classes, and they seemed fun and interesting; I had caught the bug.

However, after my mother passed away, I left property management altogether. It was time for me to shift careers. Although I enjoyed working in real estate, I didn't like the sales aspect or the many unpleasant run-ins with ruthless agents. So instead, I went to work for Catholic Healthcare West in the finance department of a hospital my grandfather helped found many decades before. I was proud to walk the halls of an organization devoted to helping people, made possible by the grandfather who helped me.

By day, I worked at a job I found rewarding, and by night, I studied to become an appraiser. With my learning disability, it was by far the most academically rigorous goal I had ever set for myself. Nevertheless, I kept working at it. I completed a 2,000-hour internship with the San Mateo County Assessor. In 2001, I passed my exams and became a certified real estate appraiser, then a certified property tax appraiser in 2003. I also worked for the San Mateo County Tax Collector and eventually struck out on my own as an independent appraiser.

As an appraiser, I was a woman in a man's world. It could still be challenging even with all my experience, but I could not imagine doing anything else. I felt good building things, making money, and being self-sufficient.

It was an eighteen-year ordeal, but I did it—and I learned something about myself in the process. When I set out to achieve a goal, I don't give up. If I am told to get from A to B, it does not matter if it takes me decades. I will get there. I inherited that dogged determination—some might call it stubbornness—from my mother and grandfather.

My grandfather's road was not easy, even though he made it look like it was. His work ethic—the same one that drove me—motivated him to advance in his career in the same way I aspire to improve myself. He always reached for the next step. I will never match his achievements, but his example constantly encourages me to keep pushing on.

I was proud to do everything that could be done to a house: I had built them, I had knocked them down, I had appraised them, and I had sold them. But that was not the end of my story.

Even after becoming an appraiser, I did not stop setting goals for myself. Neither did I stop working towards my vision for a fulfilling life, whether that was building a dream home—which I did in Burlingame in 2000—becoming healthier and more educated, starting a business, or rescuing myself from the terrifying situations life has thrown me in. I was not content unless I was working towards a goal.

A nearly fatal medical error when I was forty-seven years old helped me set a new goal. In 2010, a chiropractor adjusted my left knee to give me a greater range of motion. However, I got much more than that: the procedure caused enough swelling to form blood clots. Without emergency surgery to remove the clots, I would have died. As if that wasn't traumatic enough, when my half-sister Liza found out about my condition, she marched into the hospital and told my physicians I was "crazy" to try to prevent them from treating me. Fortunately, they did not listen to her.

After I recovered from the ordeal, I renewed my commitment to personal development. I took a page from my grandfather's book and enrolled in leadership courses. In the years since, I sought to put the lessons I learned into practice. To that end, I also took college courses on criminal justice. Rectifying injustice within my family became a common thread in my life from the moment I tried to protect my mother from my father. An underdog myself, I always rooted for the little guy.

ABSOLUTE POWER CORRUPTS ABSOLUTELY

Little did I know when the phone rang on Halloween 2013 that my half-sisters were about to come back into my life. I had not spoken to Linda since a conflict between our daughters years before, so I was shocked to hear her voice on the other end of the line. I was even more taken aback by her strange request: would I pick her up at her condo in San Bruno? I didn't even know she had moved there.

Even after everything she, Liza, and Laurel had put me through, she was still my sister. I hopped in my car. When I saw her, she insisted we drive around an apartment building my grandfather had owned while she looked for her bottle of alcohol. I held my tongue and appeased her. No surprise, we didn't find it, and when she climbed back into my car, I took her home with me.

From that day on, I took care of her—no one else would. Our half-sisters and her children did not want the responsibility. By that point, she was suffering from addiction to both alcohol and opioids. She had been in a twelve-step rehab program but could not bring herself to move past the fourth step: forgiving her physically and emotionally abusive father.

For the next four months, I did my best to keep her safe. It wasn't easy. She would drink a quart of vodka a day, and sometimes, she would run away from my home, book a hotel room across the street from a liquor store, and drink herself into a stupor. On those days, my daughter and I would drive around for hours desperately looking for her. Other times, she would pass out in my driveway, and I would have to call the fire department because I was unable to physically pick her up. She constantly cycled in and out of the hospital.

When I confronted her about the opioids, she assured me she "only" took OxyContin, not heroin. I also learned that I was the only one of my siblings not addicted to pain pills and alcohol. When she was lucid enough for conversation, she spoke only about how much pain she was in and how much she wanted to die. It hurt to hear her speak like that.

On the afternoon of February 24, 2014, I returned home from running errands and saw Linda sitting at the dining room table with her head down. I sighed, assuming she had passed out again. But when I took a closer look, I saw her face was blue, and as I lifted her head, liquid came out of her nose. I called 911 and tried to revive her, but it was too late. She was gone. She was only fifty-three.

While Linda stayed with me, I frequently updated her daughter, Liza, and Laurel on her condition. They knew exactly what her condition was. However, after she died, they blamed me for her death and refused to allow me to pay my respects at the funeral. It broke my heart all over again. No good deed went unpunished in my family.

While she was alive, Linda begged me to take our sisters to court over their mismanagement of the family trust fund. As a single mother who struggled with substance abuse, Linda depended on distributions from the family trust fund. According to Liza and Laurel, because she did not have a college degree, a profession, or money, she was unworthy. They held her in contempt and did not want anything to do with her. As trustees of the family trust fund, they were not shy about wielding their power to make Linda's life—and mine—more difficult.

When Linda passed away, I was reminded of just how short life is. Her death gave me the clarity to realize I wanted to go out with a bang, not a whimper. And that bang would force me to conquer not only my shy nature but my fear of my half-sisters. Even as an adult, they frightened me; no matter how far I had come, whenever I saw them, I would revert to the terrified five-year-old girl whose sister was going to sit on her. For justice to be served, I would have to take them to task—and court—and hold them responsible for the damage they had done to our inheritance. I had come full circle from protecting my mother physically to protecting her legacy and my grandfather's from Liza and Laurel. Once again, I set out to be the watchdog, this time by telling our story.

However, before I could do any of that, I had a lot of learning to do. So, just like when I studied to become an appraiser, I buckled down and went about educating myself in the finer points of the laws governing trust funds, trustees, and beneficiaries.

In my family, my mother and her sister Diva were the original trustees of my grandfather's trust fund. Their responsibilities passed to their oldest children when they passed away or, in my aunt's case, when she retired and moved into a nursing home.

Today, Liza, Laurel, and our cousin Rick serve as trustees. I am next in line to be a trustee.

Unfortunately, I discovered through my research that as a beneficiary, I had few rights. Among them were the right to distributions as outlined in the document; the right to enough information about the trust's administration to know how to enforce my rights; the right to detailed, annual accounting; and the right to petition the court for a trustee's removal if they failed to act in our best interests.

I exercised my right to that accounting of my family's trust fund, even though I had to go to court to get a hold of it. When I dug into the details of the trust's financial situation, what I found made my blood boil and my heart sink. Great power really did come with great responsibility. The documentation showed that Liza abused her power as a trustee and shirked her responsibilities.

From the beginning, she managed the fund for the benefit of the trustees, not the beneficiaries. She treated it like her own piggy bank: she paid herself an annual trustee fee of close to $100,000 and gave herself an 8 percent raise—every year. In addition, funds from the trust financed her cross-country flights to New York. Liza certainly did not extend the same courtesy to us beneficiaries. For twenty-five years, she refused to increase our monthly trust allowance. Some months, I was lucky to get my monthly check. She refused to use direct deposit, and I lost count of how many times she "forgot" to sign my checks.

Whenever possible, Liza used the trust fund to make my life more difficult. For example, she purposefully withheld information about a property swap in which the trustees traded real estate in New York for a property in Las Vegas. As a result, I filed an unnecessary tax return in New York, wasting both my accountant's time and my money.

When my mother was a trustee, she worked hard to ensure the trust fund generated a profit. Liza, in contrast, was a poor financial steward. I discovered the trustees put property on the market for significantly less than market value—they might as well have given it away. Likewise, she set rents on trust-held properties at far below market value. As an appraiser, I knew that devalued our property and, thus, the value of our trust fund.

Liza's management was rife with other conflicts of interest. Rather than soliciting bids for maintenance and repair projects on trust-owned properties, she contracted with her favorite vendors, including our cousin and fellow trustee, Rick. She also inappropriately proposed working on out-of-state real estate deals with former vendors.

Vendors were not the only area in which she was on the wrong side of the law. She used distribution funds to pay off the principal mortgage on property owned by the trust. Ironically, she also rented to family members—the same practice she criticized my mother for engaging in nearly thirty years ago. However, Liza couldn't claim she didn't know better. It was never about what my mother did wrong; it was about Liza's greed. All of her decisions were calculated to further her interests at the expense of the beneficiaries.

In addition to her responsibilities as a trustee, Liza was chairwoman of the board of the bank my grandfather founded. Her role was to represent the family's interests, for which she was compensated. Are those the interests she represented? Think again. She relished the power and control the position afforded her, and she was not afraid to wield it. Her greed and sense of entitlement drove her to use insider information to buy stocks at low prices, as well as secure a position at the bank for her son—a role he was later dismissed from.

She was not the only greedy Angelost. God help anyone who owed Laurel money. Poor Linda made that mistake once. One day while she was living with me, Linda needed to repay Laurel $2,800 for a loan she had made to Linda's son. I took her to the bank while she was on the phone with Laurel, who screamed at her the entire time. The bank teller and just about everyone else in the vicinity could hear every word she said as Linda sobbed hysterically. I was so embarrassed—and so angry.

In my family, as in many others, it was taboo to talk about money. We swept any discussion of our financial situation under the rug. However, I was not going to let these injustices slide any longer. Armed with my hard-won knowledge of my family's circumstances and the law, I gathered my courage started working with a lawyer to send the trustees a cease-and-desist letter. The letter asked them to acknowledge the hell they put our mother through, rectify their conflicts of interest, and increase trust-held properties' rents over the next five to ten years so that they catch up with market value. The trust fund must once again be managed for the benefit of the beneficiaries, not the trustees.

The letter was a kick in the teeth to Liza and Laurel, but there was nothing unreasonable about my demands. Justice and the law were on my side. As my mother's protector, I had to become my sisters' keeper. The responsibility challenged me like nothing else since I became an appraiser. However, just like on that journey, I pursued this goal with the same determination and would not rest easy until I secured my family's legacy.

PEACE AT LAST

As the years went by, I devoted my time and energy to my personal development, my daughter, my grandson, and our well-being. However, there were some wounds that time alone couldn't heal. I was in a dark place after Linda died. In combination with the lingering grief from the deaths of my mother and Bill—who had died at the age of fifty-three, after years of battling drug and alcohol abuse—I began a quest for answers.

I started my search in religion. I was raised Catholic and believed with every fiber of my being that God loved us and had a mission for each of us to fulfill. I studied the Bible extensively and learned to pray not for material things but for guidance and strength to accomplish my work on this earth.

Alongside religion, I pored over the science of near-death experiences. I had to know if there was a world beyond this one, a world where my mother, Linda, and my other relatives were free from their pain. So I read, watched, and listened to whatever material I could get my hands on and began to piece together the commonalities between hundreds of reports. Again and again, I found accounts of individuals whose souls were ripped from their bodies like Velcro. They saw a light, but because it was not their time, a spirit sent them back.

It wasn't just strangers' stories. Before she died, my mother received heavy doses of radiation to try to treat her cancer. One day, a tumor in her lungs began hemorrhaging blood, and the hospital called me to say she had only minutes to live. I was fortunately only a mile away, so I drove there frantically to say goodbye. She made it through that night and later told me that as she was bleeding, she saw her parents on the other side. They told her she had to come back to us—it wasn't her time yet.

Bill, too, had a near-death experience. He told me he felt his soul rise up and found himself floating above his body, watching everything happening around him. Because of their experiences and those of thousands of others, I knew there was more to this world than we could see.

When I was little, my mother would always say, "Jackie, you have a sixth sense." I always felt more in tune with God and heaven than others. Perhaps this sensitivity came from my early brush with death. I experienced strange supernatural encounters with loved ones who have passed on. After she died, my mother came to me in my dreams. I dreamed I was rowing a boat towards a light, and when I reached the shore, I saw her. She said, "I'm with you, Jackie." She was not the only one to visit me. One morning, just as the sun was coming up, I woke up from a dream and saw Bill in a rainbow of light.

A few years ago, my unanswered questions led me to make an appointment with Felix, a renowned and respected medium. I didn't know what to expect, but I quickly discovered he was the real deal. In our first session, he revealed that my father had died. I broke down right then and there. I later confirmed the truth in his words—my half-sisters had not bothered to tell me.

I met with Felix a handful of times after that first session, and every time, I learned something that made my mouth drop and left me speechless. Through him, I was able to communicate with members of my family who have passed on to the other side. They finally gave me clarity and understanding on many issues I struggled with my entire life. It was both exciting and sad to repair my relationships in this way.

During my sessions with Felix, both my father and my ex-husband apologized for the pain they caused me. I was especially grateful that my daughter, who came to a session with me, had the opportunity to speak with her father. Linda and my mother, too, expressed remorse for what I had suffered, and I tried to comfort them just as much as they comforted me.

I learned that souls on the other side want their loved ones to know that they are looking out for us and working hard to make our lives better. Unlike in life, I could trust what my family members on the other side said—they couldn't lie. They might not tell me the whole truth, or they spoke in riddles—and they certainly did not give me winning lottery numbers—but they told me what I need to hear. Sometimes, it felt like I had more support in heaven than on earth. It comforted me to know they were happy and on my side in a way they never could be on earth.

In my journey, I found that we need hope for a better future. If we lose that, we're in trouble. Felix gave me that hope, as well as a vision for my life and faith that I could turn my suffering into something good for the world. Through him, I found the courage and confidence to heal from my painful past and look ahead to a brighter future.

Part of that process was researching, writing, and publishing a book about my grandfather's life. For twenty years, I wanted to tell the world his incredible story. However, the naysayers—and my own insecurities—told me it would be foolish to even try. However, Felix helped me understand that my grandfather chose me to record his triumphs and hardships and carry on his legacy.

I took it one step at a time. If appraisers know one thing, it is research. Before I wrote the first word, I spent an entire year researching our family history, both in the United States and Italy. It might not have taken me eighteen years, but it was a grueling process. However, in the end, I published *The Family Bank: The Life and Times of Americco L. Lagomarsino.* I am proud to have achieved that part of my mission on this earth. Now, I seek to do the same thing by telling my own story. Regardless of if anyone else shares my beliefs, my long, winding spiritual journey has brought me to a better place.

I am thankful for that peace every day of my life.

EPILOGUE
PHOENIX RISING FROM THE ASHES

When I charged into my parents' bedroom to protect my mother all those years ago, I never could have imagined how much strength and courage I would need to break the abusive patterns of my childhood. However, because my grandfather and mother showed me a way to discipline without resorting to violence, I knew it was possible. I started therapy to learn how to parent without hitting and have spent the last thirty years proving they were right.

Guided by their examples, I raised my daughter with all the love, respect, and care they poured into me. Today, we strive to pass on those values to my grandson. We teach him emotional intelligence and ask him to reflect on how a situation makes him feel. Instead of hitting people or being destructive, we help him manage his emotions in a healthy way.

I know firsthand how difficult that can be. There are days when the trauma of my past and the battles I continue to fight weigh heavily on me. I struggle daily with anxiety, depression, and post-traumatic stress disorder. However, I meet those challenges with a smile on my face, just like my grandfather. I strive to live each day with a positive attitude; nothing good ever comes from a bad attitude. A lifetime of witnessing the negative examples of family and friends who have lost their way has shown me what can happen if I slip up—I don't want to lose my professional license or end up in prison. I am proud that I have not become my own worst enemy. I hope the strategies I use to keep myself balanced can guide others along the same path.

By keeping myself physically, mentally, and emotionally healthy, I work to overcome my burdens without succumbing to violence or addiction and harming myself and the people who care about me. For my body, I eat well and exercise regularly. For my mind, I am committed to attending therapy and taking the medication that keeps my mental health strong. I also have a challenging career and stimulating pursuits outside of work.

After the media attention around OJ Simpson's trial in the mid-1990s, I volunteered in a shelter for survivors of domestic abuse. While there, I taught kids how to play computer games. When I saw how happy they were whenever I walked through the door, I felt immense pride in being able to make at least a little bit of a difference in their lives. It was among the most rewarding things I had ever done. It also made me feel grateful for my own life, warts and all. Perspective is everything: there is always someone who has it worse than I do.

And for my soul, I surround myself with the family I have created, who love and support me whether or not we share blood. Life has taught me that material things come and go. All the money in the world cannot solve the hardest problems. It couldn't save my mother from cancer.

When the chips are down, relationships are what sustain us. I spent years trying to make my half-sisters love me and many more years nursing the wounds caused by their contempt. If they didn't love me, I thought, maybe I didn't deserve anyone's love. Perhaps I was not good enough for people who took more than they gave.

It was the memory of my grandfather's love that kept me going over the years. His example gave me hope that not everyone is as cruel as my siblings and that good people do exist. My best advice for anyone overcoming challenges like mine is to find the people who bring you joy and support you unconditionally. Run as fast as you can from anyone who brings you down.

Those of us who have suffered abuse, whether as children or adults, know that we're never truly safe from it. We wrestle with it our entire lives. Writing my grandfather's story and now mine has transformed my perceptions about my experiences. I could not comprehend how much I endured until I sat down to record it.

Despite the sadness in my life, I am not a victim or a martyr; I am a proud survivor. I realize now how easily my story could have ended differently, whether in addiction, like Linda; greed and bitterness, like Liza and Laurel; or abuse, like my father. By tracing the forks in my road, I can see more clearly all the times I have risen like a phoenix from the ashes to overcome obstacles in constructive, rather than destructive, ways. Just like my grandfather, I have made the best out of my circumstances, and that knowledge has helped me heal.

When I was younger, I wished someone would take me by the hand and shown me how to conquer my fears and get my message out. But there comes a time when we have to fight for ourselves to move forward and find healing and peace. I hope my example can pave the way for someone else traveling through the dark places I have been through myself.

My journey is not over, not by a long shot. I have a ways to go before justice is served within my family, and I won't rest easy until my mother and grandfather's legacy is safe for my daughter and grandson. That mission gets me out of bed every day, in spite of the bumpy road I have traveled to get there. I do not wish my experiences on anyone. However, if my story gives hope to someone struggling with domestic violence, financial injustice, rejection, or family turmoil, my challenges will have been worth it. If my story inspires someone to stand up for themselves, I will not have been a victim. And if my story can help even one person start their own healing process, I will have achieved my purpose.

I believe if I can see it, I can be it! Everyone has the power to make their lives better. All I have to do is visualize a picture in my mind. With hard work and time, I am right where I need to be in my mind's eye. It is my third eye, that gut feeling. I can never stop listening to my inner voice; it will keep me grounded and sane. And never say never again! Just when I think I am safe? I think again!

www.ingramcontent.com/pod-product-compliance
Lightning Source LLC
Chambersburg PA
CBHW050751160726
48004CB00002B/505